From The Staff Of GDW

DESERT SHIELD FACT BOOK ™

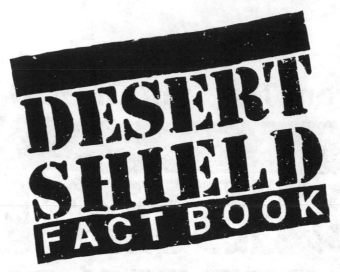

The wall map provided is a portion of JNC (Jet Navigation Chart)-35,
a 1:2,000,000-scale map prepared by
the Defense Mapping Agency Aerospace Center.

Desert Shield Fact Book™ is GDW's trademark name
for its information book about the Persian Gulf Crisis.

Written and Researched By: Frank Chadwick.
Additional Research: Loren Wiseman and the staff of GDW.
Art Direction: Amy Doubet.
Graphic Design and Production: Steve Bryant,
    LaMont Fullerton, Keith Ganske.
Additional Production: Marc Miller, Darlene File, Steve Olle,
    Julia Martin.
Printed By: Command Web Offset, Inc., Secaucus, N.J.

SINCE 1973

P.O. Box 1646
Bloomington, IL 61702-1646

CONTENTS

DESERT SHIELD FACT BOOK

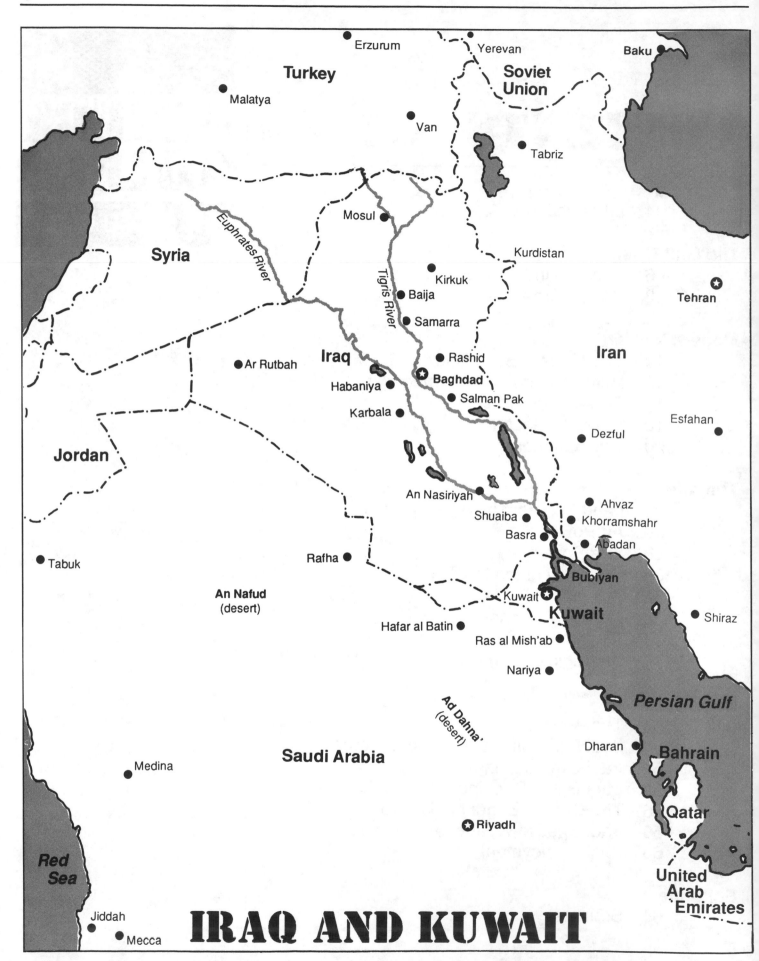

IRAQ AND KUWAIT

THE GULF CRISIS
FOREWORD

DESERT SHIELD
FACT BOOK

This is a book designed to help the average man or woman better understand military developments in the Persian Gulf. We have had two goals in putting it together: to compile the largest body of up-to-date and reliable information on the military aspects of Desert Shield available, and to present it as clear and concise manner as possible. It is intended to be a sort of guidebook through the often confusing and highly technical-sounding realm of military affairs.

The book spends some time explaining technical subjects such as armor penetration and fire control systems, and hopefully clears up some foggy areas here. But more importantly, we hope readers come away from the book with an understanding of the basic *logic* behind most military equipment and procedures. Military science is, at its best, a fairly simple, logical, and direct approach to the solution of military problems, and the average person is fully capable of grasping the basics of it. However, the first step in doing so is overcoming the feeling that it is a hopelessly complex, arcane, black art, the secrets of which are understandable only to a select few.

If this book helps to dispel that notion then it has served all of us well.

WHAT THIS BOOK IS NOT

This book is not a political statement. One of the unique advantages Americans enjoy (that Iraqis do not) is the ability to freely participate in the political process. This book, however, is not intended to be part of the political debate in any way. It is a factbook, as the title states, and is as politically neutral as the author could make it. If readers are unable to determine the author's strongly-held political opinions as to the course of this crisis and our response to it, then that is another way in which the book has succeeded.

This book is not a treatise by an expert on Mid-Eastern affairs. The author is not an "expert" at all in any of the conventional senses of the word. Instead, this is a book by a researcher. It presents what the average person would find if he or she spent months researching this particular topic, given a strong beginning background in military affairs.

This book is not an expose of secret or sensitive information. All data presented in this book is taken from open sources. No sensitive material is exposed, no secrets let out of the bag. There are no "scoops" anywhere in its pages, except perhaps insofar as it presents information which has been published but largely overlooked or misunderstood.

This book is not an attempt to predict events in the Persian Gulf. In that sense, it is not really intended for the armchair general. One of the least-understood aspects of generalship outside of the military may be the most important, but is certainly among the least glamorous. That aspect is logistics, the supplying of armies. That is an area in which there simply isn't sufficient information generally available to make a genuine military plan.

For example, how many tons of fuel will each US division consume a day? What is the fuel lift capacity of the trucks actually in place in Saudi Arabia? What volume of traffic can each of the roads crossing from Saudi Arabia to Iraq and Kuwait actually sustain? Without an answer to fundamental questions like that, it is impossible know which of the general outline plans argued back and forth are even possible.

Instead of trying to predict what will happen *in advance*, this book is designed to help the reader understand events *as they unfold.*

A NOTE ON SOURCES

A variety of reference works were consulted in the preparation of this book. The most important of these, however, was is the bi-weekly military affairs newsletter For Your Eyes Only. It is the best summary of military current affairs available, in this author's experience, and readers interested in updating the information in this factbook could do no better than to subscribe to this periodical. This is an unpaid endorsement, and there is no connection between either the author or the publisher of this book with the newsletter. We have provided subscription information for those interested on the back page of this book.

BACKGROUND: THE GULF CRISIS

The Persian Gulf is the location of some of the world's oldest trade routes. For as long as there have been trade routes, there have been conflicts over them. Likewise, ever since there have been borders, there have been border disputes. Oil is a relatively recent bone of contention, but one of global importance.

Both Iraq and Kuwait were once part of the Ottoman Turkish Empire, which was broken up by the League of Nations after the defeat of the Ottoman Empire during the First World War. Iraq had an ancient tradition of national independence dating back to the time of the Babylonians, but over the centuries had been part of the Persian and Turkish empires. Kuwait was one of a number of small semi-independent emirates ruled by the Ottomans.

The Al-Sabah family founded the Emirate of Kuwait in 1759, but the area had been annexed by the British in 1899. The British administered Iraq under a mandate from the League of Nations after WWI. In effect, this made them colonies in all but name: Britain controlled their economy and their diplomatic relations, and was responsible for their defense. The mandate ended in 1932, when a king was installed by the British. Kuwait remained a British protectorate until after the Second World War, finally acquiring independence in 1961.

Oil was discovered in the region in the 1930s, but WWII prevented its exploitation until 1946. Both Iraq and Kuwait were founding members of the Organization of Petroleum Exporting Countries (OPEC,) a coalition formed to control prices and impose limits on annual production of oil.

IRAQ

Iraq was a viable nation-state before oil. It now has a fair system of agriculture, mineral deposits in the northern mountains, and some industry. Iraq is almost self-sufficient agriculturally, and its industrial capacity gives it much more economic viability than Kuwait. In many ways, it is a potentially dangerous powerhouse, especially if it continues its alleged nuclear program.

The British-imposed limited monarchy was destroyed with the assassination of King Feisal II in 1958, and a republic was established, but no elections have been held since that time. The present provisional constitution has been in effect since the Ba'ath (renaissance) Socialist Party of Iraq (BPI) overthrew the government of then Prime Minister Kassem, and took power in 1968. Saddam Hussein, the current president, was an important member of the BPI since 1959, and held several important government positions from 1968 onward, becoming president after disposing of his rivals in 1979.

Iraq has had border conflicts of varying intensity with almost all of its neighbors since the end of the mandate, ranging from diplomatic notes exchanged with Syria to the Iran-Iraq War. Iraqi troops even entered Kuwait briefly in 1973

KUWAIT

Kuwait has effectively no resources besides oil: most of the land is arid desert, and the country is dependant on foreign imports for all of its food and some of its drinking water. Ninety percent of Kuwait's export income is from petroleum and petroleum products, the remainder is largely from re-exports.

Kuwait attained its independence from Britain in 1961, when the United Kingdom largely withdrew its influence from the Persian Gulf. It has been ruled by the Al-Sabah Emirs, under a constitution adopted in 1963 (although certain electoral provisions were suspended in 1976) since that time.

ORIGINS OF THE CONFLICT

The origins of the Iraq-Kuwait conflict go back for generations. Many of the borders in the region were arbitrarily imposed by the British during the 1930s. A major point of continual conflict has been the large Rumaila oil field, which straddles the Iraq-Kuwait border.

Basically, Iraq claims that Kuwait has been pumping more oil from the Rumaila field than it is entitled to. Iraq claims that Kuwait ignored OPEC production ceilings in the late 1980s, selling more than its quota on the open market, and consequently costing Iraq millions in lost revenue. Finally, Iraq claims that Kuwait was once part of the old Ottoman province of Basra, that during the Ottoman empire and continuing under the British mandate both Iraq and Kuwait were administered from Baghdad, and thus Kuwait should rightfully have been made a part of Iraq in 1932, with the establishment of the present Iraqi state.

Further points of contention are Warba and Bubiyan Islands, which block direct access to the Iraqi port of Umm Qasr from the Persian Gulf. Iraqi-bound oil tankers must pass through the narrow confines off these islands, and their possession by another nation was a continuing irritant to Iraq.

Finally, in 1990, Iraq demanded

that Kuwait cede its portion of the Rumaila field to Iraq, and demanded $2.5 billion in reparations for the oil removed from it illegally, as well as another $14 billion in lost Iraqi revenue due to quota violations. Iraq also demanded cancellation of $12 billion in loans made by Kuwait to Iraq during the Iran-Iraq War. The Kuwaitis refused to discuss the matter, and Iraq began massing

troops in July as a means of forcing Kuwait to the negotiation table.

As it turned out, the negotiations lasted less than an hour. Many observers believe that Iraqi demands were set excessively high to provide a premise for an invasion. Whatever the case, according to several eyewitness accounts, the Iraqis have begun systematically looting Kuwait of everything that isn't nailed down.

KUWAIT

The Gulf Crisis DESERT SHIELD FACT BOOK

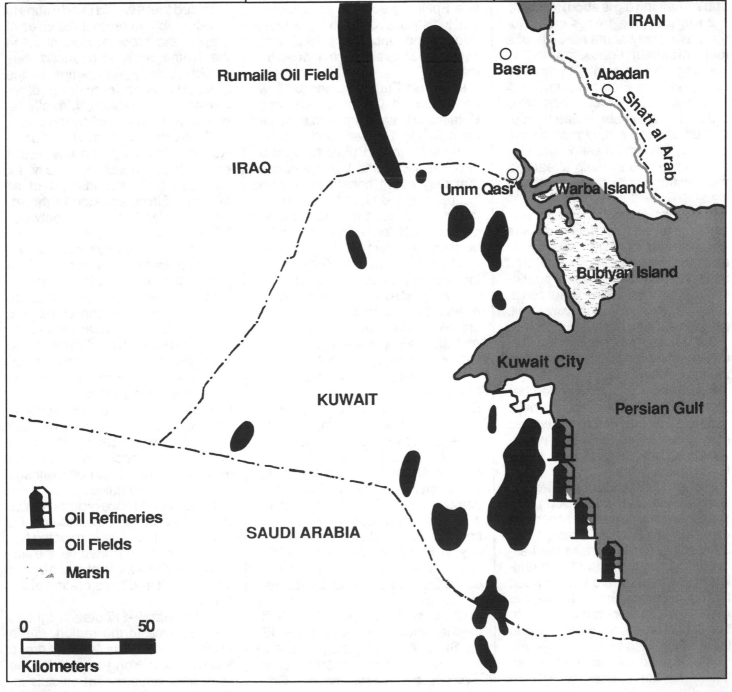

IRAN

Rumaila Oil Field

Basra

Abadan

Shatt al Arab

IRAQ

Umm Qasr

Warba Island

Bubiyan Island

Kuwait City

Persian Gulf

KUWAIT

SAUDI ARABIA

Oil Refineries

Oil Fields

Marsh

0   50

Kilometers

A CHRONOLOGY
DESERT TIMETABLE

This is a partial chronology of events through December, 1990.

31 July: Increased delivery orders to the White House staff tip off one Washington DC pizza parlor that something big is about to break.

2 August: Iraqi troops enter Kuwait, ostensibly at the request of a local group in opposition to the reigning Emir. Kuwait City falls by noon, and the Emir flees to Saudi Arabia. US carrier *Independence* is ordered to the Arabian Sea to support US vessels in the Persian Gulf.

3 August: Britain sends two frigates to join one warship already in the region, and France sends a warship as well.

4 August: Resistance at the palace in Kuwait City finally ceases after heavy fighting, but uncoordinated resistance by isolated units and individual soldiers continues. Elsewhere, the EEC agrees to an embargo on Iraqi and Kuwaiti oil, as does Japan.

5 August: Iraq begins the formation of 11 new divisions for use in the impending crisis.

6 August: A US tactical bomber squadron (F-111s) moves to Turkey, ostensibly on "previously scheduled maneuvers." The UN votes worldwide economic and military sanctions against Iraq.

7 August: The Saudis agree to allow US aircraft and troops into Saudi Arabia. Several American warships (the carrier *Saratoga*, the battleship *Wisconsin*, and the helicopter carrier *Inchon* with a battalion of marines) leave port headed for the Persian Gulf. The carrier *Eisenhower*, scheduled to return to the United States from its station in the eastern Mediterranean, moves to the Arabian Sea instead. Egypt allows the "Ike" to pass through the Suez Canal.

8 August: American F-15s and paratroopers take up positions in Saudi Arabia. The troop build-up is named Desert Shield. Italy, Germany and Spain agree to provide bases and logistical support to US forces. Greece announced that US aircraft could transit its airspace headed for the gulf.

9 August: Turkey agrees to allow an increased US presence, and Britain and France agree to send air units to the Persian Gulf region, along with ground units to protect airbases. Syria and Iran announce that they might consider sending troops, and the USSR announces that it might send a contingent as part of a UN force. Iraq closes its borders and "urges" foreign embassies in Kuwait to merge their facilities with those in Baghdad.

10 August: Congress is informed of the US troop deployment. The US 3rd Air Cavalry regiment and 11th Air Defense Brigade are put on alert for deployment to Saudi Arabia.

11 August: Egyptian and Morroccan troops begin arriving in Saudi Arabia. Iraqi troops kill a British oil worker while he attempts to escape across the Saudi border.

12 August: President Bush orders what amounts to a blockade (although it is not called that, since doing so is technically an act of war), and USAF Sgt. John Campsi becomes the first American casualty in Saudi Arabia, in a vehicle accident. A brigade of the 101 Airborne Division embarks for the region.

13 August: A brigade of the 24th mechanized Division leaves the US for Saudi Arabia by sea, and advance units of two Egyptian armored divisions begin crossing the Red Sea into the Arabian Peninsula by ferry. British ships join US vessels in enforcing the anti-Iraq embargo. The French dispatch a carrier (the *Clemenceau*) and Pakistan announced that it would send troops to Saudi Arabia to protect the cities of Mecca and Medina. Australia and the Netherlands announced they would contribute warships to the blockade. Americans and other foreigners in Iraq are formally labelled as "restrictees" by the Iraqis.

15 August: The US carrier *Kennedy* leaves port a few weeks earlier than scheduled, heading for the Mediterranean instead of its original training mission in the Atlantic. Several incidents between US and Iraqi aircraft occur, but no shots are fired. Iraq offers a number of concessions to Iran in return for a peaceful border with that nation.

16 August: Saddam Hussein, President of Iraq, threatens that "thousands of Americans would return home in body bags" if war erupts.

18 August: Iraq formally announced that some Europeans would be forced to remain in Iraq until the threat of foreign invasion ceased. US frigates fired warning shots at Iraqi tankers, which did not stop, and proceeded into harbor at Yemen (where the Yemenis refused to allow them to unload).

19 August: France orders its ships to join in enforcing the embargo. An Iraqi peace initiative is rejected because it does not involve the immediate withdrawal of Iraqi forces from Kuwait and a restoration of the Emir.

20 August: F-117 stealth fighters are deployed to the region, and a Marine amphibious landing group leaves Hong Kong bound for the Gulf. Iraqi government officials insist that any solution to the Kuwait crisis must be linked to a settlement of the Israeli/Palestinian question.

22 August: Nearly 50,000 US reservists and Guard troops are called up or placed on alert, mostly support and logistical personnel. The advance guard of the 24th Mechanized arrives in Saudi Arabia, as do the first units of the US Third Army headquarters.

24 August: The *Wisconsin* and its associated vessels arrive in the area. Two thousand Jordanian troops embark for Saudi Arabia.

25 August: The UN votes to allow "minimal force" to be used in enforcement of the embargo, and the Secretary General announces that he will visit Jordan and perhaps Iraq in an attempt to negotiate a settlement. The first American diplomatic dependents are allowed to leave.

28 August: American tanks, IFVs, and SP artillery of the 24th Mechanized Division begin unloading in Saudi Arabia. Other tanks are en route with units of the 1st Cavalry Division and the 197th Brigade. Up until this time, the only American tanks in the country were light M551s of the 82nd Airborne Division's tank battalion and USMC M60A3s.

6 September: An American civilian is shot and wounded in Kuwait, while trying to evade capture by Iraqi soldiers. Troop levels deployed to the Gulf area reach 100,000.

10 September: The US formally called upon the European nations to send troops to the Persian Gulf, even token contributions.

28 September: The UN Security Council votes to seek separate solutions to the Kuwaiti and Palestinian questions, a major defeat to Iraq's attempts to link the two. Troops of the French Foreign 1st Mechanized Battalion arrive.

30 September: The USSR announced that Soviet troops would participate in actions against Iraq, but only under UN auspices. More French Foreign Legion troops arrive (elements of the 2nd Mechanized Battalion and the 21st Marine Battalion), bringing the total French

ground troops to 4,000.

2 October: The carrier *Independence* enters the Persian Gulf.

11 October: Tanks of the American 3rd Armored Cavalry regiment, 2nd Armored Division, and 1st Cavalry Division continue unloading in Saudi Arabia.

14 October: Iraq again lets it be known that it will withdraw if it is allowed to retain the islands of Warba and Bubiyan, which block Iraqi access by water to the Persian Gulf.

15 October: President Bush suggests that war crimes trials might follow a resolution to the crisis, and Marines in Saudi Arabia conduct their first training maneuvers.

16 October: First significant antiwar demonstration occurs. President Bush is heckled by protestors.

19 October: President Bush reaffirms that Iraqi forces must unconditionally withdraw from Kuwait before any negotiations can begin.

20 October: Small antiwar demonstrations in a number of US cities.

22 October: President Mubarak visits Egyptian troops in Saudi Arabia.

23 October: General Colin Powell, the US Chairman of the Joint Chiefs of Staff, visits troops in Saudi Arabia. Iraq released 14 aged or sick American detainees.

30 October: The American 4th Marine Brigade begins exercises in Oman.

1 November: Iraq announces relatives of hostages will be allowed to visit during Christmas holidays.

2 November: Three captured French soldiers were repatriated through the French embassy in Baghdad.

4 November: American Secretary of State Baker visits American troops in Saudi Arabia.

5 November: Baker meets with the Saudi King Fahd and command arrangements for combined American/Saudi forces are worked out. A poll showed that over half of Americans favored an American attack on Iraq if sanctions did not force Iraqi troops out of Kuwait.

8 November: An additional

140,000 troops are ordered to reinforce those already participating in Desert Shield, in order to create an "offensive military option."

13 November: The battleship *Missouri* and its associated ships depart for the Persian Gulf.

14 November: The first of 200 M1A1 tanks (with 120mm rather than 105mm guns) arrive in Saudi Arabia.

15 November: Operation Immanent Thunder, an amphibious multi-service training exercise, begins near the southern border of Kuwait. It is widely believed to be the cover for an invasion, but this proves not to be true.

18 November: Iraq announces that all foreign "detainees" will be released over a three-month period starting at Christmas. Operation Immanent Thunder is delayed due to inclement weather, making the exercise too risky for a peacetime operation.

19 November: Iraq announces that it will move an additional 250,000 troops into Kuwait and mobilize another 150,000 reservists in response to recent American actions.

20 November: President Bush arrives in Saudi Arabia to visit troops over the Thanksgiving holiday. Shortly thereafter, a UN resolution passes, endorsing "limited military action" if sanctions have no effect by 15 January 1991.

2 January: Information cutoff date for this handbook.

THE MODERN
BATTLEFIELD

The modern battlefield is, in basic terms, no different than any other in history. Because of the greater capabilities of modern weapons, it appears to be, and in fact is, much more complex. However, this complexity is because of the large number of different types of combats taking place over a wide area at the same time. Each of these combat events, examined separately, has a logic of its own which is easily understood.

The main difference between the battlefield of today and that of World War II is that in World War II close air support and mechanized vehicles were usually the exception to the rule. Most battles were fought between leg-mobile infantry forces. When Germany invaded the Soviet Union in 1941, the Blitzkrieg attack was conducted by 148 combat divisions. But of these, only 19 were armored divisions; the rest were infantry; all but a half-dozen walked, their artillery towed by horses.

By comparison, not a single division of the 3rd Army in Saudi Arabia will walk into battle. A few will fly, either in helicopters or troop transports. Others will be carried ashore by armored amphibious combat vehicles. The vast majority will ride to battle in fully-armored tracked vehicles.

CAN THE TANK SURVIVE?

This is probably the wrong question. Try asking this one instead. "If it can't, what can?"

Tanks form the backbone of all modern armies for the simple reason that they are the most survivable and the most lethal system capable of engaging in mobile warfare available. They are not invulnerable, but no weapon systems

ever have been throughout history. Any system can be defeated by some other system, given the right circumstances. But tanks remain extremely effective, and are the most easily measured yardstick of a unit's combat potential.

While armed helicopters may supplant them in this role, they have not yet done so, for the simple reason that they cannot yet carry the ammunition that a tank does or linger in the area of the battle as long. As a result the helicopter can deliver a sharp blow, but cannot take and hold ground.

CAN INFANTRY SURVIVE?

Yes.

Infantry will always have a place on any land battlefield. So long as an infantryman is alive and resisting in a foxhole, that foxhole belongs to that soldier's side. Dismounted infantry is extremely difficult to dig out of entrenchments, built up areas, or even rugged ground. Furthermore, dismounted infantry in the desert tends to disappear in the heat shimmer beyond a couple hundred meters, which gives it a tremendous advantage over vehicle-mounted troops.

Enemy forces will have to either send tanks in to clean them out, or send in their own dismounted infantry. In the first case the defending infantry's light anti-tank weapons can be used to get close-range flank and rear shots on the tanks. In the second, it boils down to a straight infantry fight.

Why go in an clean them out? Why not just ignore them? Because where there are infantrymen there may be long-range anti-tank missiles and there are certainly forward observers for artillery.

FIELD ARTILLERY

As armies have become increasingly mechanized, artillery has lost the ability to dominate the battlefield it once had. Most mobile forces are carried in armored vehicles proof against artillery fragments.

A new generation of munitions is restoring artillery as an important component of the combined arms team, however. The two most important types of HE rounds used by Allied forces in the Gulf are ICM and FASCAM. Neither of these are available to Iraqi forces.

ICM (Improved Conventional Munitions) rounds are filled with dozens of 40mm shaped charge grenades. These are devastating to infantry or gun crews in the open, and so are ideal rounds for silencing towed artillery units. (3000 of Iraq's 3500 field guns are towed instead of self-propelled). Of equal importance, their HEAT warhead also has the ability to disable lightly armored vehicles, such as APCs and IFVs, and can even damage tanks given a lucky hit.

FASCAM (Field Artillery Scatterable Mines) rounds allow an artillery unit to quickly lay antitank and antipersonnel minefields several kilometers away from the closest friendly troops, a tremendously valuable ability in mobile warfare. This gives a rapidly moving mechanized force the ability to screen its own flanks and blunt enemy counterattacks by sowing mine barriers in the path of advancing mobile reserves.

CLOSE AIR SUPPORT

The Soviet Air Force, once the leading exponent of close air support, has completely abandoned the concept and switched to deep strike missions. Their stated reason for doing so is that they do not believe that any aircraft, including their own, can survive in their own forward air defense zone. They may have a point.

Fortunately, Iraq does not have nearly the density or quality of air defense systems as does the Red Army, and theirs will be much more vulnerable to Allied countermeasures. Therefore, close air support, particularly from A-10 ground attack aircraft, will play an important part in a potential conflict in the Gulf.

It is eloquent evidence of the US Air Force's own reluctance to embrace the close air support mission that they have recently signed on to an agreement to turn all A-10 aircraft over to Army command (once the current crisis is resolved and there is time to reorganize the force structures.)

Once the air war starts, the Air Force estimates that it will be able to generate approximately 700 air sorties a day. (A sortie is a single flight by an aircraft, and is a convenient measure of overall air effort.) The Navy will generate about 100 sorties per aircraft carrier. The Marines will generate between 150 and 200 sorties a day.

COMBAT HELICOPTERS

A potentially revolutionary development since Vietnam has been the proliferation of the armed helicopter. Once considered a novelty, armed helicopters now appear in virtually every nation's arsenal. They have yet to be used in large numbers by both sides in a conventional war, however, and so it is likely that growth of technology in this field has outstripped that of doctrine. That is, most armies have real helicopters, but only unproven theories as to how to use them.

That notwithstanding, the odds are that their use will be tremendously important. When used in comparative small numbers in Lebanon and the Iran-Iraq War, they were often decisive battle-winning instruments. If used in battalion and brigade concentrations, they may become war-winners.

AIR DEFENSE

Generally speaking, there are three types of air defense weapons in widespread use, guns, platform SAMs, and MANPADS.

Guns are rapid-fire high velocity guns, usually ranging in caliber from 20mm to 57mm. Because of the rapid transit time of tactical aircraft and the short effective range of guns,

they are of limited usefulness against jet attack aircraft unless massed in very dense concentrations. They are much more useful against armed helicopters.

Platform SAMs are large surface-to-air missiles launched from fixed mounts or vehicle chassis. The US Improved HAWK is one of the best platform SAMs in use, although the Soviets produce a wide variety of weapons in this category as well.

MANPADS (Man-Portable Air Defense Systems) are shoulder-fired SAMs like the Soviet-built SAM-7 and the US Stinger. Stinger is a remarkably effective weapon in this category, with as good a range and a better hit chance than many platform SAMs.

GADGETS VERSUS GUTS

Most of the above discussion concentrates on equipment: It is easier in many ways to explain the workings of machines in battle than it is the workings of men. Historically, though, the relative quality of weapons has been a much less significant predictor of victory than has the relative quality of manpower. Outstanding troops with fair equipment will beat fair troops with outstanding equipment most of the time.

The important role that good equipment plays is to enable good troops to do their job that much better, and to preserve the lives of good troops to let them fight again in subsequent battles.

In World War Two, the 3rd US Army was commanded by General George S. Patton, Jr., a commander known for his dashing style and aggressive spirit. As the troops deployed in Saudi Arabia today are again commanded by the 3rd US Army, it is worth remembering what General Patton had to say on this subject. His words ring as true today as they did forty-five years ago.

"The Americans, as a race, are the foremost mechanics in the world. America, as a nation, has the greatest ability for mass production of machines. It therefore behooves us to devise methods of war which exploit our inherent superiority. We must fight the war by machines on the ground, and in the air, to the maximum of our ability... While we have ample manpower, it is too valuable to be thrown away."

MODERN MILITARY JARGON & SYMBOLS

The military has a language and a symbology all its own. This section will do its best to explain some of the more common words and phrases used, and to make them more intelligible to the average person.

UNIT SIZES

Armies are constructed of a hierarchy of units. Many small units are organized into larger and larger units.

Squad: A unit consisting of 6-12 soldiers, usually led by a sergeant. Squads are the basic building block of a unit, and in most armies the squad is the smallest unit.

Section: A section is a unit intermediate in size between a squad and a platoon. A section contains 15-30 soldiers, and is usually led by a senior sergeant. The British Army uses the term section for squad.

Platoon: A platoon consists of 3-4 sections or squads (40-50 soldiers), plus a platoon leader (usually a lieutenant) and an assistant platoon leader (a senior sergeant).

Company: A company consists of 3-5 platoons, plus a headquarters, and is usually commanded by a captain.

Troop: A troop is a company-sized unit of cavalry. In British usage a troop is a platoon-sized armored or mechanized cavalry unit. When British and US units operate together, this can be a source of confusion. (See also *squadron*.)

Battery: A battery is a group of artillery pieces of some kind, and is usually company-sized in terms of

the number of personnel involved.

Batallion: A battalion consists of 3-5 companies plus a headquarters company. It is usually commanded by a lieutenant colonel.

Squadron: In the US Army a squadron is a battalion-sized unit of cavalry. In the British Army it is a company-sized unit of tanks or armored cars.

Regiment: A regiment consists of a number of battalions, usually 3-5, plus a headquarters unit. It is usually commanded by a Colonel. In many armies (including those of Britain and France) a regiment means a battalion.

Brigade: A brigade consists of a number of battalions, usually 3-6. It is usually commanded by a colonel or a brigadier general (1 star).

Division: A division consists of a number of brigades or regiments (usually three), plus smaller supporting units (battalions or companies). It is usually commanded by a major general (2 stars). The division is the largest unit for which a formal table of organization exists.

Corps: A corps contains several divisions, the exact number depending upon its intended mission, plus smaller supporting units. A corps is usually commanded by a lieutenant general (3 stars).

Army: An army consists of several corps, plus supporting units. It is usually commanded by a general (4 stars).

UNIT SYMBOLS

The organizational diagrams in this book make use of a standard set of military symbols, which are explained here. Fundamentally, the system consists of a rectangular box symbol identifying the troop type, a unit size indicator atop it, and various numbers and letters giving more information about the unit. Nationality is to the left of the rectangle, and the unit's identifying number or other data is to the right.

In the sample shown, the rectangle with the oval in it represents an armored unit. The two Xs atop it indicate that it is a division. The US to the left of the rectangle give nationality, and finally, the 3 to the right indicates that the unit is the US 3rd Armored Division. Multiple units are represented as shown by the example, by "stacking" several rectangles (the symbol represents three artillery battalions).

Sometimes unit type symbols are combined: note, for example that the mechanized infantry symbol combines the infantry and armor symbols.

	UNIT SIZE		Leader
Infantry	XXXX	Army	General (4 stars)
Armor, Tank	XXX	Corps	Lieutenant General (3 stars)
Mechanized Infantry	XX	Division	Major General (2 stars)
Airmobile Infantry	X	Brigade	Colonel or Brigadier General (1 Star)
Airborne Infantry	III	Regiment	Colonel
Heavy Weapons	II	Battalion	Lieutenant Colonel
Armored Cavalry, Recon, Armored Car	I	Company or Battery	Captain
Cavalry	●●●	Platoon	3-4 Squads or sections, 40-50 men, commanded by a lieutenant
Marine Infantry	●●	Section	2-3 squads, 15-30 men, commanded by a senior sergeant.
Artillery	●	Squad	6-12 men, commanded by a sergeant.

Mortars

Self propelled Artillery

Air Defense Artillery

Multiple Rocket Launcher

Antitank Artillery or ATGM

Self-Propelled Antitank Artillery or ATGM

Engineers

Army Aviation

Multiple units

Motorized Unit

Motorized Infantry

US ⬭ 3

Motorized Recon

Sample: US 3rd Armored Division

UNIT SYMBOLS
Based on NATO standards

DESERT SHIELD
FACT BOOK

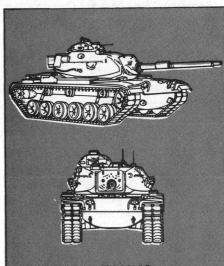

WHAT IS A TANK?

One of the most commonly made errors in military reporting is confusion of tank with armored vehicle. A tank is a tracked, heavily-armored vehicle whose principal purpose is to carry a heavy direct-fire cannon. Often reporters mistake anything with a turret for a tank. The Soviet-built BMP is often called a tank, as is the US Bradley IFV. Although they are tracked vehicles and have turrets, they fail to qualify as tanks on three grounds. First, they are lightly armored. Second, they carry a comparatively small gun. Third, their main purpose is not to carry the gun system, but rather to transport infantry. The M109 self-propelled howitzer is also sometimes mistaken for a tank, but it doesn't qualify because it is lightly armored and its gun is for indirect fire, not direct fire.

MILITARY TERMS

The military needs a special vocabulary because it deals with special equipment and activities. These are some of the words they use.

AFV

Armored Fighting Vehicle. A vehicle intended to engage in combat, which means it is armored and armed. AFV covers several types of vehicle, including tank, APC, CFV, and IFV.

APC

Armored Personnel Carrier. An armored personnel carrier is an AFV whose primary mission is to transport infantry around the battlefield. It is usually lightly armored (to protect the passengers from small arms fire and shell fragments).

ARM

Anti-Radiation Missile. ARMs are missiles equipped to seek out and home in on radar emissions. They are primarily used by airplanes to attack enemy antiaircraft radars.

Armored

This means that the vehicle is equipped with protection for its passengers and crew. Heavily armored means that a vehicle is capable of resisting main gun hits. Lightly armored means that a vehicle is capable of resisting hits from small arms fire and shell fragments.

ATGM

Anti-tank Guided Missile. A guided missile is a weapon that uses the thrust of a rocket motor to propel it to the target (and does so constantly throughout its flight), and is capable of making course corrections that guide it towards a target, even if that target is moving.

ATGW

Anti-tank Guided Weapon. Technically any guided warhead intended to defeat armored vehicles, including CLGP (see below). In practice, it is usually synonymous with ATGM. ATGMs and ATGWs are usually of two types: beam riders, which follow a beam of laser or infrared radiation to their target (a human has to constantly keep the beam on the target in order for the missile to guide on it), and wire-guided, which follow guidance instructions from a complex electronic sight (which also has to be kept pointed at the target).

AWACS

Airborne Warning and Control System. An aircraft-mounted radar system used to detect enemy aircraft and direct defenses to intercept them.

Blister Agent

This is a form of chemical weapon that attacks the skin of its victims, causing chemical burns. Gas masks and protective clothing will work against this weapon.

Blood Agent

This is a form of chemical weapon that must be inhaled to kill. Masks provide adequate protection against this type of weapon.

CBR

Chemical, Biological, Radiological. The military speciality concerned with these three specialized types of warfare. At times, the speciality has been called ABC (Atomic, Biological, Chemical) and NBC (Nuclear, Biological, Chemical).

CFV

Cavalry Fighting Vehicle. A type of AFV intended for scouting or recon purposes. These vehicles are sometimes called armored cars, and are lightly armored, although they may be heavily armed.

Chobham

A type of composite armor developed by the British, and incorporated into the design of the M1 Abrams tank. A diagram of Chobham armor is shown in the section discussing the M1 tank.

CLGP

Cannon-Launched Guided Projectile. This is a ballistic weapon, which means that it does not have thrust propelling it throughout its flight path, but it does have fins and a complex electronic guidance system enabling it to be guided to its target.

Direct Fire

These are weapons which shoot at targets the firer can see (although the round may not follow a straight line to get there). Some weapons may be used in both direct and indirect fire (see Indirect Fire).

EW

Electronic Warfare. The use of radar and electronics to detect, mislead, or counter enemy activity.

FASCAM

Field Artillery Scatterable Minefield. This is an artillery round containing a number of antitank or antipersonnel mines. It is a means of laying a minefield quickly and with minimal risk.

FLIR

Forward Looking Infrared. The night vision device used on allied aircraft that provides detailed images based on the heat radiated by an object. Similar in principle to thermal vision devices.

HEAT

High Explosive Anti-Tank. A type of warhead that relies on a high-velocity stream of molten metal to punch through armor. This high-speed stream of metal is generated by the burning of a a carefully shaped explosive charge.

Heavy Forces

Heavy forces are units containing tanks or combined arms teams of tanks, mechanized infantry, and self-propelled artillery. Heavy forces are capable of delivering devastating firepower, but tend to be very expensive in fuel and ammunition. They often take (and cause) heavy casualties.

ICM
Improved Conventional Munition. A form of artillery projectile containing a number of smaller grenades. At a fixed distance above the ground, the ICM shell casing fractures and the smaller grenades (sometimes called bomblets) are scattered over a wide area, exploding on contact with the ground, or at a preset height of 1-3 meters.

IFV
Infantry fighting Vehicle. An AFV intended to transport infantry on the battlefield and provide combat support with its own armor-defeating weapons as well. The American M2 Bradley and the Soviet-designed BMP are IFVs.

Indirect Fire
Indirect fire is directed against targets which the firer cannot see, usually from information received from forward observers, observation aircraft, or recon vehicles. All long-range artillery fire is indirect fire.

MBT
Main Battle Tank A heavily armored AFV carrying a large caliber main weapon, capable of participating in the most intense fighting. The US MBT is the Abrams.

Mechanized
Infantry which rides in APCs or IFVs. Such infantry can move faster, carry more and heavier weapons, and strike harder than non-mechanized infantry.

MLRS
Multiple Launch Rocket System. A weapon for launching "volleys" of several rockets at once or in rapid succession. Most MLRSs are mounted on vehicles, and are self-propelled.

MOS
Military Occupational Specialty. The specific training and experience background for a soldier. The MOS for many soldiers is simply infantryman or tank crew. For others, it is vehicle mechanic, clerk, or radar technician. There are thousands of MOS designations.

Motorized
Infantry which rides in trucks or other unarmored vehicles. The chief advantage of such infantry is speed.

MRL
Multiple Rocket Launcher. This can be another name for an MLRS, but some MRLs are towed rather than self-propelled.

Nerve Agent
A form of chemical weapon that attacks the nervous system, and can be absorbed through the skin. This is the most deadly form of chemical weapon, as a single drop on exposed skin can be fatal within minutes. Masks, and full suits are required for protection.

Platform
The navy term for any of its vessels. A ship or a submarine is a platform (for weapons).

Republican Guards
Elite troops of the Iraqi regime. They are the most reliable and best equipped forces available.

SAM
Surface to Air Missile. A missile intended to be fired at aircraft from the ground, usually incorporating some form of homing device enabling it to guide itself to its target.

Special Forces
In western usage, commando-style elite light troops designed for clandestine and unconventional missions. In the Iraqi Army they are heavily-armed assault troops.

SSM
Surface to Surface Missile. A missile intended to be fired from the ground at another target on the ground. These include both guided and unguided missiles.

Modern Warfare

DESERT SHIELD
FACT BOOK

Thermal Sights
Thermal sights make use of the heat generated by a target to detect it, even in total darkness.

Zulu
The designation for the standard Greenwich Mean Time (GMT) zone. The 24 time zones around the world are designated with alphabetic letters. In global military operations, GMT or Zulu time is used.

TANK VERSUS ANTI-TANK

Tanks protect themselves with thick armor while their opponents try to disable the tank by blowing a hole through its armor.

A variety of ammunition types are available, but all attempt to penetrate armor in the same way: A dense penetrator forces its way through the armor with kinetic energy by brute force. In conventional rounds the penetrator is solid metal, usually tungsten or depleted uranium due to their hardness. In HEAT (High Explosive Anti-Tank) the penetrator is a stream of molten metal created by the explosion of the warhead.

The penetration tables show the penetration of the main tank gun rounds, anti-tank missiles, and infantry anti-tank rocket launchers in use in the Persian Gulf. Gun penetration is influenced by several factors, the most important of which are traditionally caliber (diameter of the round) and muzzle velocity (the speed at which it leaves the gun). In the past decade, however, advances in ammunition technology have dramatically increased the performance of existing guns. A variety of different ammunition types are shown on the chart to illustrate this fact.

As a point of comparison, the German *Koenigstiger* (King Tiger, or Tiger II), thought by many to be the most powerful tank of World War II, is also shown on the charts. At that time considered to be nearly unstoppable, and with a gun that would rip through the armor of any tank on the battlefield, it serves to demonstrate how far the arts of tank protection and anti-tank warfare have progessed.

HOW ANTI-TANK ROUNDS WORK

There are a wide variety of anti-tank rounds, but two types predominate: Armor-Piercing Fin Stabilized Discarding Sabot (APFSDS) and High Explosive Anti-Tank (HEAT).

APFSDS is fired from both rifled and smoothbore guns. A finned dart-shaped penetrator is encased in a two- or three-piece sabot (SAY-bow) of a lightweight material, such as aluminum. The light weight of the round means that the powder charge accelerates it to extremely high velocities. Upon leaving the gun tube the sabot falls away, while the penetrator hurtles downrange and pierces the target's armor.

HEAT rounds can be fired from guns, but may also be the warheads of light rockets or wire-guided missiles. This is so because the round does not rely on the velocity of the projectile to generate energy. Instead, the round detonates when it hits the target.

HEAT has a *shaped charge* warhead that directs the explosion forward. A molten stream of metal blasts forward and this metal stream acts just like the solid penetrator of the APFSDS round.

For a very long time it was thought that HEAT rounds actually burned their way through armor, but engineers have now shown that the fluid dynamics equations describing penetration by APFSDS rounds also describe the penetration by the metallic jet of a HEAT round.

The advantage of HEAT is that it does not require a high projectile velocity to work, so it doesn't need a gun system to generate that velocity. Infantrymen cannot carry around a tank gun, but they can carry around a low-velocity rocket launcher with a HEAT warhead. Similarly, wire-guided missiles give infantry and light vehicles a potent long-range anti-tank capability.

The disadvantage of HEAT is that the penetrator jet is easily disrupted, degrading the ability of the round to penetrate and destroy. The two main means of disrupting the jet are Chobham armor and reactive armor.

No Iraqi tanks have been observed with reactive armor or the mounting brackets needed for its use.

The only tanks in the Persian Gulf theater using reactive armor are the M-60 tanks of the 1st Marine Tank Battalion, often shown in television news reports with their large, easily recognizable sheets of reactive armor blocks on the turret and chassis front.

Who Uses What?

Anti-Tank Guided Missiles

Hellfire: USA.

TOW: Egypt, Morocco, Oman, Saudi Arabia, UAE, Bahrain.

I-TOW: Kuwait.

TOW II: USA.

Milan: France, UK, Oman, Qatar, UAE, Egypt.

Dragon: Morocco, USA, Saudi Arabia.

AT-3 Sagger: Iraq, Syria.

AT-4 Spigot: Syria.

HOT: France, Iraq, Kuwait, Qatar, Saudi Arabia, UAE.

Swingfire: UK.

Light Anti-Tank Weapons

LRAC F1: France.

Carl Gustav: UK, Kuwait, Qatar, Saudi Arabia, UAE.

RPG-7: Syria, Egypt, Iraq.

M72A1 LAW: Morocco, USA.

LAW 80: UK.

Tank Gun Penetration at Effective Range (1000-2000 Meters)

88mm L70 (German World War II King Tiger)
- AP — 175mm

90mm F1 (many French Armored Cars)
- 90F1 HEAT — 325mm

100mm (T-55)
- BR-412 AP — 135mm
- BR-412D HVAP — 175mm
- BM-6 APDS — 265mm
- BK-5M HEAT — 380mm

105mm F1 (AMX-30, AMX-10RC)
- HEAT — 375mm

105mm L7 (M1)
- M-392 APDS — 250mm
- M-735 APFSDS — 375mm
- M-833 APFSDS — 435mm
- M-456A2 HEAT — 425mm

115mm (T-62)
- BR-5 APFSDS — 300mm
- HEAT — 450mm

120mm L11A5 (Challenger)
- APFSDS — 400mm

120mm (M1A1)
- M-829 APFSDS — 525mm
- M-829E1 APFSDS — 650mm

125mm (T-72)
- APFSDS — 450mm
- HEAT — 500mm

Antitank Guided Missile Penetration at All Ranges

- Hellfire (Range: 4000m) — 1050mm
- TOW (Range: 3000m) — 600mm
- I-TOW (Range: 3500m) — 800mm
- TOW II (Range: 3750m) — 900mm
- Milan (Range: 2000m) — 600mm
- Dragon (Range: 1000m) — 500mm
- AT-3 Sagger (Range: 3000m) — 400mm
- AT-4 Spigot (Range: 2000m) — 500mm
- HOT (Range: 4000m) — 800mm
- Swingfire (Range: 4000m) — 800mm

Light Antitank Weapon Penetration at All Ranges

- M72A1 66mm (Range: 200m) — 325mm
- LRAC F1 89mm (Range: 400m) — 400mm
- RPG-7 (Range: 500m) — 400mm
- LAW 80 94mm (Range: 500m) — 600mm
- Carl Gustav 84mm (Range: 700m) — 400mm

HIGH TECHNOLOGY
ARMOR PROTECTION

Tanks and other armored vehicles rely on armor for protection from enemy weapons. Most armored personnel carriers (APCs) have very light armor, intended only to keep out small arms fire and enemy artillery fragments. Tanks, however, have considerably thicker armor intended to defeat some or all of the enemy's anti-tank weapons.

This page presents a graphic comparison of armor protection of the main tanks in service in the region. In all cases, the value shown is the estimated average protection throughout the frontal arc of the tank (which is where most enemy fire comes from). Because heavy armor on all faces would be prohibitively heavy, tanks always have less protection on their sides and rear. Weapons unable to penetrate the front armor of the tank can still be effective if they are positioned for flank or rear shots, but this is difficult and hazardous.

All armor is listed in its equivalent to hardened armor plate. The term *equivalent* is important here, because most tanks have armor considerably thinner than the values shown. However, tank armor is usually angled against attack from the most likely direction. Extreme angles increase the chance that an enemy round will glance off, but any angling of the armor increases the effective thickness of armor that a round may penetrate.

As a rule of thumb, armor angled at 30 degrees from vertical is about 50% more effective than its nominal thickness while armor angled at 60 degrees from vertical is about twice as effective.

Note that some tanks have two different armor thicknesses shown, one for conventional rounds and a second (greater) one for HEAT rounds. These are tanks with either Chobham or reactive armor.

Reactive armor is extremely simple in principle. A number of explosive blocks are fastened to the outside of an armored vehicle; they explode when hit by an enemy high energy round. They are designed so that machinegun fire will not detonate them (at least in theory). While reactive armor has little effect on conventional armor-piercing rounds, it is very effective against HEAT rounds, as it disrupts the penetrator jet and degrades their penetration.

While the exact physics of reactive armor are still being studied, the closest explanation to date is that the explosion of the block blows its cover plate up and away at an angle while the jet is still passing through it, thus removing considerable mass from the stream itself.

The first army to employ reactive armor was the Israeli Defense Force in Lebanon. It was used

TANK, COMBAT, FULL-TRACKED, 105-MM GUN, M60A3 (TTS) APPLIQUE ARMOR

because tanks were forced to move into built up urban areas where enemy infantry anti-tank teams could easily attack with hand-held rocket launchers. The Soviet army followed suit soon after with a major effort to incorporate reactive armor arrays on its tank forces in Europe as a counter to NATO's superiority in anti-tank missiles. Soviet reactive armor, which probably has typical performance, adds about 550mm worth of protection to the tank against HEAT-type warheads.

No reactive armor blocks are believed to have reached Iraq prior to the arms embargo, and no Iraqi tanks have been observed with reactive armor or the mounting brackets needed for its use.

The only tanks in the Persian Gulf with reactive armor are the M60 tanks of the 1st Marine Tank Battalion, often shown in television news reports with their large, easily recognizable sheets of reactive armor blocks on the turret and chassis front.

REACTIVE ARMOR

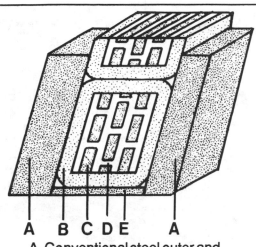

Modern Warfare

DESERT SHIELD

FACT BOOK

CHOBHAM ARMOR

Chobham armor was developed at, and named after, the Chobham Arsenal in the United Kingdom. The armor used on U.S. tanks is slightly different than true British Chobham armor, and is slightly more effective against HEAT rounds, but is constructed along identical principles.

A. Conventional steel outer and inner armor plates.

B. Aluminum or plastic inner casing.

C. Ceramic blocks.

D. Epoxy or other special glue matrix.

E. Additional armor sheet holds armor blocks in place. In some versions the blocks are held in place by bolts.

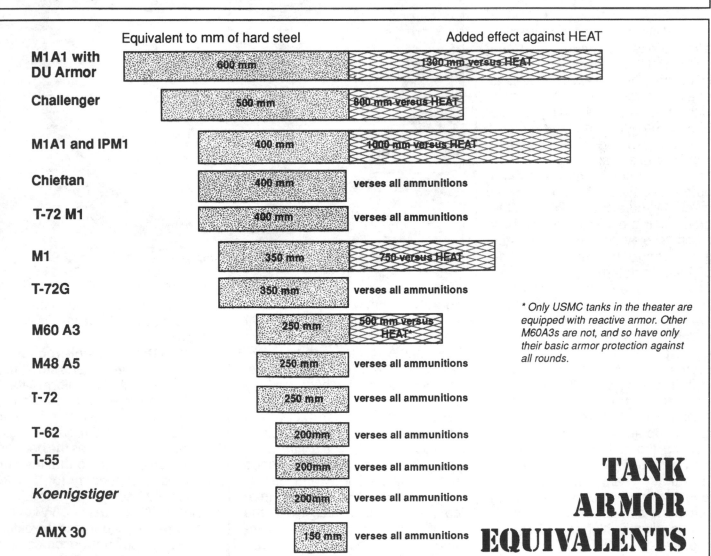

	Equivalent to mm of hard steel	Added effect against HEAT
M1A1 with DU Armor	600 mm	1300 mm versus HEAT
Challenger	500 mm	800 mm versus HEAT
M1A1 and IPM1	400 mm	1000 mm versus HEAT
Chieftan	400 mm	verses all ammunitions
T-72 M1	400 mm	verses all ammunitions
M1	350 mm	750 versus HEAT
T-72G	350 mm	verses all ammunitions
M60 A3	250 mm	500 mm versus HEAT*
M48 A5	250 mm	verses all ammunitions
T-72	250 mm	verses all ammunitions
T-62	200mm	verses all ammunitions
T-55	200mm	verses all ammunitions
Koenigstiger	200mm	verses all ammunitions
AMX 30	150 mm	verses all ammunitions

* Only USMC tanks in the theater are equipped with reactive armor. Other M60A3s are not, and so have only their basic armor protection against all rounds.

TANK ARMOR EQUIVALENTS

PROBLEMS AND SOLUTIONS
TANK GUNNERY

Hitting an enemy tank is complicated by a number of variables, and the gunner must generate a solution to each of these variables in order to achieve a hit.

Range: When a round leaves the barrel of a tank's gun, it immediately begins to fall. In fact, if a tank's gun were exactly parallel to the ground and you fired it at the same time as you dropped a similar round from the same height as the gun, both rounds would hit the ground at the same time.

The distance from a gun at which a round hits the ground when the gun barrel is parallel to the ground, is called *point blank* range. It is relatively easy to hit a tank which is within this range: All you have to do is point the gun at the tank and fire.

If the target is further away, though, you need to elevate the gun to keep the round from hitting the ground before it gets to the target. How much do you elevate it? That's the problem. It is easy to compute how much to elevate the gun for any given range to the target. The problem is determining the range. The quicker and more accurately the gunner can determine the range, the more accurate the fire.

Cant: If the gunner knows the range to the target, he simply elevates the gun the correct amount and fires. However, if the tank is canted (tilted to one side), elevating the gun will not just move it up, it will move it up and slightly to one side, causing the round to miss. If the tank is canted (and it's a lucky tank crew that can always find perfectly level ground) the gunner must somehow compensate for this by aiming slightly higher and to the opposite direction from the cant.

Crosswind: Crosswinds are not

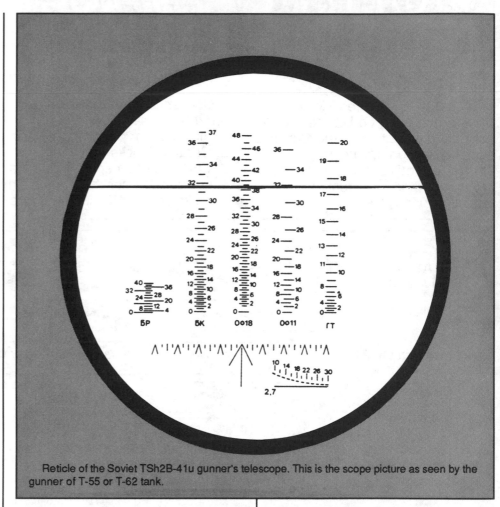

Reticle of the Soviet TSh2B-41u gunner's telescope. This is the scope picture as seen by the gunner of T-55 or T-62 tank.

a great problem when firing at close range, but at progressively longer ranges they become more and more important. Also, modern high velocity tank rounds are particularly susceptible to crosswind because they are fin-stabilized.

A crosswind pushes on all parts of a rifled round the same. As a result, it will push it to the side a little, but it won't alter its course. With a finned round, however, the wind affects the tail of the round much more than the front, and so actually twists the round. Instead of blowing it downwind, it will tend to turn it upwind.

Unless the gunner can accurately

gauge the effects of crosswinds, it is very difficult to hit a target at long range.

Barrel Droop: A tank's gun sights assume that the barrel is straight, or at least droops at a uniform rate. In combat, however, repeated firings of the gun will cause it to heat up, and as it does so the barrel begins to droop. This changes the ballistics of the gun enough so that the gunner must compensate for it or the rounds will begin to fall short.

Barrel Wear: As a gun is fired, the barrel wears out, and the older it is the more worn it becomes. This also affects the ballistics of the rounds fired from the tank.

Ammunition: Different types of ammunition fired from the same gun have different ballistic characteristics. Therefore the correct range elevation for APFSDS will cause HEAT rounds, which have uniformly lower velocities, to fall considerably short of the target.

THE SOLUTIONS

How a gunner solves the fire control variables depends largely on the type of fire control equipment he has at his disposal.

Range: The most basic range finder is the reticle range finder used on most tanks of Soviet design. A small part of the sight is devoted to the range-finding reticle which the gunner places over the target tank. (See the example of the T-62 sight reticle shown to the side.) The bottom line is aligned with the ground and the point at which the curved line on the top of the reticle intersects the top of the tank indicates the range. The reticle is graduated in 200-meter increments and is set up for a 2.7-meter tall target. If the tank is hull-down, or lower in silhouette than 2.7 meters (as the M1 is), or if it falls between two range bands, the gunner must estimate.

With a stereoscopic or coincidence range finder, like that found on most versions of the T-72, the gun sight has two lenses which, when correctly focused on the target (much like with a camera), will tell the gunner the range.

With a laser range finder available on virtually all allied tanks, but probably only on the handful of T-72Ms available to Iraq, the gunner places the sight on the target and triggers the laser, which then instantly provides the range accurate to within a meter.

Once the gunner has the range, he must set the sight for the correct range and then traverse and elevate the gun until the target is centered on the aiming point. In U.S. tanks, however, all of this is done automatically by the ballistic computer. Once the sight is on the

target and the gunner triggers the laser, the computer receives the range and then elevates the gun until it is at the correct position relative to the sight. The target remains centered in the gunner's sight the whole time, as a result, making his job much easier.

Cant: On tanks without ballistic computers, the gunner takes a good guess at the effects of gun tilt and tries to make mental allowances for them. On Allied tanks the ballistic computer automatically measures the cant of the tank and feeds the proper correction into the gun sight once the range measurement is done.

Crosswind: On tanks without ballistic computers, the gunner makes his best guess as to what effect the wind will have and tries to mentally generate a correction for it. This is one reason that Soviet tanks suffer such poor long-range accuracy. Most Allied tanks, however, are equipped with wind sensors which feed crosswind speed and direction information to the ballistic computer, which again automatically feeds the corrections to the gun sight.

Barrel Droop and Barrel Wear: On tanks without computers, the gunner ignores barrel droop and barrel wear, as there is nothing he can do about it. If a round falls short, he aims a little higher and tries again. To minimize barrel droop, many tanks (including the T-72, but not the T-55 or T-62) incorporate a thermal barrel sleeve, which helps maintain the barrel at a constant temperature.

The ballistic computers on allied tanks actually measure the current barrel droop and remember how many rounds have been fired from the gun tube, and correct the gun accordingly.

Ammunition: For gunners without ballistic computers, there are separate parts of the sight picture for each type of ammunition, and the gunner uses the appropriate set of range elevation lines. In tanks with ballistic computers, however,

the gunner just punches the button corresponding to the correct ammunition type before taking the range check and the computer does the rest.

High Tech versus Low Tech

A question sometimes asked is, *Are our soldiers well-enough educated to understand all this complex, high-tech equipment?* Most soldiers justifiably find this question insulting. They are, after all, very highly motivated and well-trained professional soldiers; they are not morons.

Beyond this, the question illustrates how little the person understands modern weapon systems. High-tech systems, such as the ballistic computers and laser range finders on modern U.S. tanks, are far *easier* to use than similar systems of Soviet design with which the Iraqi army is equipped. This enables U.S. tank gunners to fire first and hit with the first round. In most tank battles that will be the critical survival edge.

THE ALLIED ARMIES
LAND POWER

The following units are currently deployed in the Persian Gulf Theater or are on their way as of January 5, 1991.

CENTRAL COMMAND
Gen. Norman Schwarzkopf (USA)

UNITED STATES 3RD ARMY
Lt. Gen. Yeosock (USA), assisted by Lt. Gen. Prince Khalid bin Sultan (Saudi Royal Army)

SAUDI I CORPS
Saudi 1st Division
    4th Armored Brigade (AMX-30)
    20th Mech Brigade
    8th Armored Brigade (M60A3)
Saudi 2nd Division
    — Mech Brigade
    — National Guard Bde
Kuwaiti Division
    35th Armored Brigade (4,000 men, 32 Chieftain tanks, 70 M84 (T-72) tanks)
    — Mech Brigade (4000 men, 40 M84 (T-72) tanks)
    — Mech Brigade (4000 men, 40 M84 (T-72) tanks)
Peninsula Shield Force: weak division-sized group from UAE, Qatar, Oman, and Bahrain.

EGYPTIAN CORPS
Egyptian 7th Mech Division
    8th Tank Brigade
    11th Mech Brigade
    12th Mech Brigade
Egyptian 4th Armored Divisions
    2nd Tank Brigade
    3rd Tank Brigade
    6th Mech Brigade
Syrian 9th Armored Division
    52nd Tank Brigade
    53rd Tank Brigade
    43rd Mech Brigade
French 6th Light Armored Dvn
    1st Foreign Legion Armored Regt (AMX-10RC)
    1st Regiment de Spahis (AMX-10RC)
    2nd Foreign Legion Mech Rgt
    21st Marine Mech Battalion
    — Mechanized Battalion
    — Tank Rgt (AMX-30 B2)
    68th Artillery Regiment
    11th Marine Artillery Rgt
    6th Engineer Rgt
    5th Cbt Helicopter Regiment
    7th Cbt Helicopter Regiment
Separate Brigades
    Egyptian — Parachute Brigade
    Syrian — Parachute Brigade
    African Brigade
        Senegalese Infantry Bn (500 men)
        Niger Infantry battalion (481 men, CO is Colonel Amadou Seyni)
        Moroccan Mechanized Battalion (reinforced battalion from the 6th Regiment. Strength 1700 men. equipped with M113 APCs.)

BRITISH
1st Armoured Division (will serve under U.S. 3rd Army Command reinforced with a U.S. armored or mechanized brigade, probably 3rd Brigade, 3nd Mech Division, which has been serving as a separate brigade)
    7th Armoured Brigade
        Royal Scots Dragoon Guards (57 Challengers)
        Queen's Royal Irish Hussars (57 Challengers)
        1st Staffordshire Infantry (45 Warriors)
        40th Field Regiment (24 M109 SP 155mm howitzers)
        664th Helicopter Sqdn (9 Lynx)
        10th Air Defence Battery
    4th Armoured Brigade:
        14/20 King's Hussars (43 Challengers in 3 squadrons)
        1st Royal Scots (45 Warriors)
        3rd Royal Fusiliers (45 Warriors)
        23rd Regiment, Royal Engineers
        46th Air Defence Battery (36 Javelin shoulder-fired SAMs)
        2nd Field Regiment (24 M109 SP 155mm howitzers)
    Division Troops
        39th Regiment, Royal Engineers
        16/5 Queen's Royal Lancers (24 Scorpions, 24 Scimitars, 12 Strikers)
        32nd Heavy Artillery Regiment (16 M109 SP 155mm howitzers, 12 M110 SP 203mm howitzers)
        4th Army Aviation Regiment (24 Lynx with TOW, 12 Gazelle helicopters)
        39th Heavy Artillery Regiment (12 MLRS)
        12th Air Defense Regiment (24 tracked Rapier SAMs)

U.S. XVIII CORPS

1st Cavalry Division

1st Brigade: 2 tank, 1 mechanized infantry, 1 artillery battalions

2nd Brigade: 2 tank, 1 mechanized infantry, 1 artillery battalions

1st ("Tiger") Brigade, 2nd Armored Divisions: 2 tank, 2 mechanized infantry, 1 artillery battalions

Division Troops: 1 MLRS battery, 1 air defense artillery, 1 engineer, 1 cavalry, 1 helicopter gunship battalions

24th Infantry Division (Mech)

1st Brigade: 1 tank, 2 mechanized infantry, 1 artillery battalions

2nd Brigade: 2 tank, 1 mechanized infantry, 1 artillery battalions

197th Separate Mechanized Brigade (The $1.97): 1 tank, 2 mechanized infantry, 1 artillery battalions, 1 cavalry troop

Division Troops: 1 MLRS battery, 1 air defense artillery, 1 engineer, 1 cavalry, 1 helicopter gunship battalions

82nd Airborne Division

1st Brigade (325th Parachute Regiment): 3 airborne infantry battalions

2nd Brigade (504th Parachute Regiment): 3 airborne infantry battalions

3rd Brigade (505th Parachute Regiment): 3 airborne infantry battalions

Division Troops: 1 light tank, 1 air defense artillery, 3 105mm towed artillery, 1 engineer, 1 recon, 1 helicopter gunship, 1 transport helicopter battalions

101st Air Assault Division

1st Brigade (187th Air Assault Regiment): 3 airmobile infantry battalions

2nd Brigade (327th Air Assault Regiment): 3 airmobile infantry battalions

3rd Brigade (502nd Air Assault Regiment): 3 airmobile infantry battalions

Division Troops: 1 air defense artillery, 3 105mm towed artillery, 1 engineer, 1 helicopter gunship, 3 transport helicopter battalions

Corps Troops

3rd Armored Cavalry Regiment: 3 armored cavalry squadrons, 1 air cavalry squadron, 1 artillery battalion

12th Aviation brigade: 5 helcopter battalion (gunship and transport)

18th Corps Aviation Bde: 3 helicopter battalion (gunship and transport)

18th Field Artillery Brigade: 4 artillery battalions

III Corps Artillery (attached to XVIII Corps)

7th Field Artillery Brigade: 4 artillery battalions

212th Field Artillery Brigade: 4 artillery battalions

214th Field Artillery Brigade: 4 artillery battalions

11th Air Defense Artillery Group: 3 to 5 air defense artillery battalions

36th Engineer Group

The Allies

DESERT SHIELD

FACT BOOK

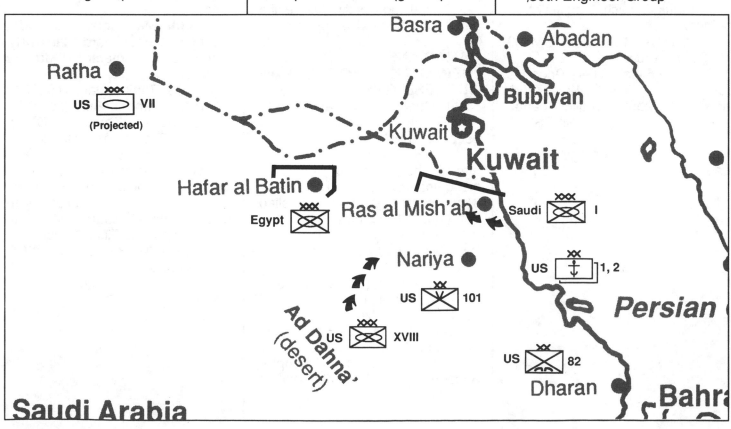

U.S. VII CORPS

3rd Armored Division

6 tank, 5 mechanized infantry, 1 engineer, 1 air defense artillery, 3 artillery, 1 cavalry, 2 helicopter gunship, 1 transport helicopter battalions, 1 MLRS battery

350 M1A1, 330 M2/M3, 72 M109, 8 MLRS

1st Armored Division

6 tank, 4 mechanized infantry, 1 engineer, 1 air defense artillery, 3 artillery, 1 cavalry, 2 helicopter gunship, 1 transport helicopter battalions

350 M1A1, 280 M2/M3, 72 M109, 8 MLRS

2nd Armored Cavalry Regiment

3 armored cavalry, 1 air cavalry, 1 artillery battalions

125 M1A1, 115 M3, 24 M109, 25+ helicopters

1st Brigade, 2nd Armored Division (to reinforce 1st Mech Division):

2 tank, 1 (or 2) mechanized infantry, 1 artillery battalions

115 M1A1, 75 M2, 24 M109

3rd Brigade, 3rd Mech Division: (to reinforce British 1st Armoured Division)

1 tank, 2 mech, 2 artillery battalions

56 M1A1, 150 M2/3, 48 M109

Corps Troops

Three Field Artillery Brigades (drawn from 17th, 41st, 42nd, 72nd, and 210th), about 4 artillery battalions each: mix of 155, MLRS, 8", and LANCE.

19th or 130th Engineer Brigade

US MARINE CORPS

1st Marine Division (Expeditionary Force)

1st Marine Expeditionary Bde

7th Marine Expeditionary Bde

4th Marine Expeditionary Bde (afloat)

13th Marine Expeditionary Unit (Battalion) (afloat)

1st Marine Tank Battalion (M60A3)

2nd Marine Tank Battalion (M1A1)

2nd Marine Division (Expeditionary Force)

5th Marine Brigade

6th Marine Brigade

4th Marine Tank Battalion (M60A3)

8th Marine Tank Battalion (M60A3)

USMC Units
Not in the Persian Gulf
(Reserve Force)

9th Marine Expeditionary Bde: Okinawa

37th Marine Expeditionary Unit: Western Mediterranean

1st Regimental Landing Team: Forming from reservists.

Several additional separate rifle battalions deployed worldwide.

CANADIANS
(DEPLOYMENT NOT CERTAIN AT PRESS TIME)

4th Canadian Mechanized Bde

Royal Canadian Dragoons (56 Leopard 1 MBTs)

1er Bataillon, Royal 22e Regiment ("The Van-Doos")—mechanized infantry with M113 APCs, 81mm mortars, and self-propelled TOW antitank vehicles

2nd Battalion, Princess Patricia's Canadian Light Infantry—mechanized infantry, as above

1st Regiment (battalion), Royal Canadian Horse Artillery—24 M109 SP 155mm howitzers

4th Combat Engineer Regiment (battalion).

No. 444 Tactical Helicopter Squadron—11 OH-58A observation helicopters

ADDITIONAL U.S. FORCES TO DEPLOY FROM CONTINENTAL UNITED STATES (CONUS)

1st Mech Division (less 1st Brigade based in Europe)

2nd Brigade: 2 tank, 1 mech infantry, 1 artillery battalions

3rd Brigade: 2 tank, 1 mechanized infantry, 1 artillery battalions

Division Troops: 1 engineer, 1 air defense artillery, 1 cavalry, 1 helicopter gunship, 1 transport helicopter battalions (engineer and cavalry battalions each minus 1 company deployed in Europe)

230 M1, 130 M2, 48 M109, 8 MLRS

4th Mechanized Division (2 brigades, to absorb 155th Armd Bde)

155th Armored Brigade, Mississippi National Guard: 2 tank (M1), 1 mechanized infantry, 1 artillery battalions

5th Mechanized Division (2 brigades, to absorb 256th Mech Bde)

256th Mechanized Brigade, Louisiana National Guard: 1 tank (M1), 2 mechanized infantry, 1 artillery battalions

Separate Brigades and Battalions

48th Mechanized Brigade, Georgia National Guard: 1 tank (M1), 2 mechanized infantry, 1 artillery battalions

1-263 Tank Battalion (SCNG): M1A1 to augment 48th Mech Bde

2-252 Tank Battalion (NCNG): M1A1 for 2nd Armored Division

142nd Field Artillery Brigade (Arkansas National Guard) (2 M110 SP 203mm howitzer battalions)

1-158 Artillery Battalion (Oklahoma National Guard): MLRS to augment 142nd Field Artillery Brigade. (Only MLRS battalion in NG force structure)

OTHER ALLIED UNITS

Saudi Arabia

Royal Guards Brigade (in Rihyad)

— Tank Brigade (in Tabuk)

— Mech Brigade (on Western Iraqi Border)

— Mech Brigade (on Yemeni Border)

— Parachute Brigade

National Guard Brigade(s)

Kuwait

Helicopter Detachment (12 Gazelle AH, 6 Puma UH, 4 Super Puma naval helicopters. Gazelle will have HOT, Super Puma will have Exocet)

Moslem Allied Units

— Bangladeshi Brigade (in Mecca) (6,000 men)

— Egyptian Infantry brigade (in UAE)

— Syrian Para-Commando Battalion (in UAE)

— Pakistani Bde (5,000 men)

European Allied Units

1st French Hussar (in UAE) (270 paratroopers, airfield defense)

Bulgarian volunteer unit (forming, probably medical)

Czech hospital unit and chemical decontamination platoons

Other

New Zealand hospital team

The Allies
DESERT SHIELD
FACT BOOK

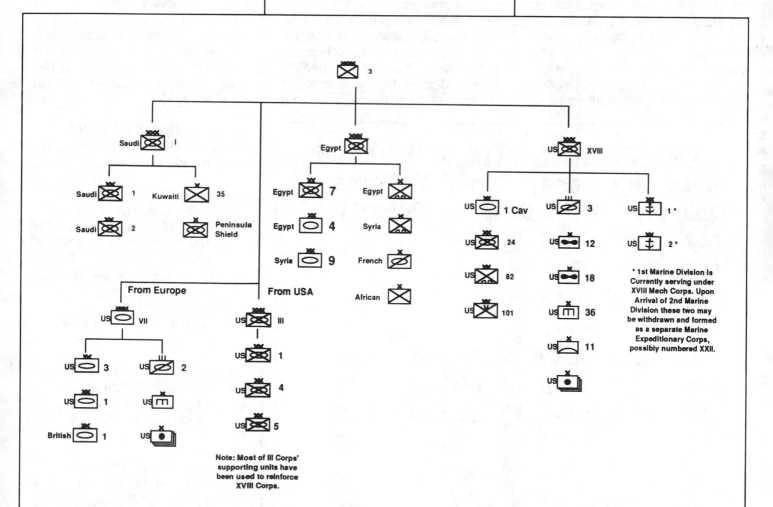

Note: Most of III Corps' supporting units have been used to reinforce XVIII Corps.

* 1st Marine Division is Currently serving under XVIII Mech Corps. Upon Arrival of 2nd Marine Division these two may be withdrawn and formed as a separate Marine Expeditionary Corps, possibly numbered XXII.

3RD ARMY STRENGTH as of Dec 15, 1990

BATTLES IN THE SKIES
AIR POWER

One significant advantage the Allies have in the Persian Gulf is their air power. The Allied air forces outnumber the Iraqis by a margin of roughly three to one. This edge is dramatically increased by the vast technical superiority of Allied aircraft, a generally higher level of training (with U.S. Navy pilots in particular considered among the finest in the world), and a complete monopoly on airborne warning and control (AWACS) planes.

Virtually all scenarios outlining the likely course of hostilities begin with a massive, sustained Allied air offensive. A possible initial Allied air of-fensive might go like this:

On the first day of hostilities, Allied aircraft will make night penetration missions aimed at destroying all Iraqi air bases, command centers, and as many air defense sites as can be identified. These will be spear-headed by F-117 Stealth Fighters and F-111 strike aircraft and may be conducted in conjunction with a massive navy cruise missile strike. Also high on the priority list will be Iraqi ballistic missile launchers capable of delivering chemical strikes. B-52's will deliver Air Launched Cruise Missiles from a distance. A majority of Iraqi air defense units which use radar guidance will probably be knocked out in the first day of the offensive. Nevertheless, the large number of optically sighted air defense guns will continue to be a threat throughout the conflict.

On later days the air offensive would shift to Iraqi ground forces, principally reserves, and A-10 "Warthog" attack aircraft would be used extensively in the tank-busting role. Entrenched Iraqi infantry will be more difficult, and less lucrative, targets for air strikes, and so allied airpower would be used to deny Iraqi armor operational mobility, even at night.

THE ALLIED AIR FORCES
The Allied air forces have approximately 1500 combat aircraft.

Royal Air Force (UK)
36 combat aircraft
1 sqdn 12 Tornado F3 air supe-riority fighters: Dharan, Saudi Arabia
1 sqdn 12 Tornado GR1 strike aircraft: Tabuk (N.W. Saudi Arabia)
1 sqdn of 12 Jaguar fighter-bombers: Bahrain
1 flight 4 Nimrod maritime patrol aircraft: Oman

Canada: 18 combat aircraft
409th Tactical Fighter Sqdn 18 CF-18 fighter bombers: Qatar
1 sqdn 12 C-130 transports: Qatar

France: 32 combat aircraft
1 sqdn 8 Mirage F1 fighter-bombers: Saudi Arabia
1 sqdn 8 Mirage 2000 air supe-riority fighters: Saudi Arabia
1 sqdn 8 Jaguar fighter-bomb-ers: Saudi Arabia
1 sqdn 8 Jaguar fighter-bomb-ers: Qatar

COMPARING THE AIRCRAFT

Allied Air Forces		Iraqi Air Force
Quantity	Best	Quantity
144	F-14	
190	F-15	
162	F-16	
12	Tornado F-1	
8	Mirage 2000	MiG-29 18
210	F/A-18	MiG-25 25
37	Mirage F-1	Mirage F-1 30
98	F-5	MiG-23 70
48	F-4	MiG-21 70
28	Jaguar	J-7 80
	Worst	

In a one-on-one battle, the better-rated aircraft can be expected to win.

This chart only rates air-to-air combat capabilities of various aircraft.

Italy: 8 combat aircraft
1 detachment 8 Tornado GR1 strike aircraft, drawn from elements of the 6th and 35th Squadrons.

Netherlands: 18 combat aircraft
315th Fighter Sqdn with 18 F-16 fighter-bombers (The squadron exchanged several pilots with the 313th Squadron so that all pilots shipped to the Gulf had at least 2 years experience.)

Belgium: 0 combat aircraft
1 sqdn 8? C-130 transports.

New Zealand: 0 combat aircraft
1 medical detachment with 3 C-130 transports.

Saudi Arabia:
279 combat aircraft
1 sqdn 72 Tornado GR1 strike aircraft (24 each)
3 sqdn 72 F-15 fighters (24 each)
4 sqdn 98 F-5 fighter-bombers (24 each)
2 sqdn 37 Strikemasters (18 each)

Kuwait: 25-30 combat aircraft
1 sqdn 29 Mirage F1 fighter-bombers (15 still operational from Saudi airfields)
1 sqdn 30 A-4 Skyhawk ground attack aircraft (perhaps a dozen still operational from Saudi airfields)

United States Marine Corps:
128 combat aircraft
1st Marine Air Wing
60 AV-8B Harrier ground attack aircraft
48 F-18 fighter-bombers
20 A-6 strike aircraft
2nd Marine Air Wing
40 AV-8B Harriers
48 F-18 fighter bombers
20 A-6E strike aircraft

United States Air Force:
510 combat aircraft
(not counting Reserve and Air National Guard reinforcements)
Initial Forces (August)
1st Tactical Fighter Wing
2 sqdn 48 F-15C fighters

4th Tactical Fighter Wing: Oman
2 sqdn 48 F-15C/E fighters
363rd Tactical Fighter Wing
2 sqdn 48 A-10 ground attack aircraft
401st Tactical Fighter Wing (from Spain, 24 aircraft still there): Qatar
2 sqdn 48 F-16 fighters
35th Tactical Fighter Wing
2 sqdn 48 F-4G fighter-bombers
Separate Squadrons
1 detachment with 5 E-3 AWACS planes
1 sqdn 14 F-111 strike aircraft
1 sqdn 24 F-117 stealth fighters
Bomber Wings
50 B-52 Bombers
December Reinforcements
(ordered 9 November):
5 combat air wings (total)
4 sqdn 96 F-16 fighters
1 sqdn 22 F-117 stealth fighter
1 sqdn 22 F-15E fighters
1 sqdn 24 A-10 ground attack aircraft
1 sqdn 24 RF-4C recon aircraft
1 sqdn 18 F-111 strike aircraft
1 sqdn 24 KC-135R tankers
US Air Force Reserve & National Guard Call-Up
(3 December)
926th Air Force Reserve Tactical Fighter Group (A-10)
169th South Carolina ANG Tactical Fighter Group (F-16A)
174th New York ANG Tactical Fighter Wing (F-16A ground attack)
152nd Nebraska ANG Tactical Recon Group (RF-4C)

United States Navy:
More than 400 combat aircraft (See the listing under Sea Power.)

THE IRAQI AIR FORCE
Despite nearly a decade of war with Iran, Iraqi pilots have virtually no experience in air-to-air combat. This is because the Iranian Air Force, starved for replacement parts and aircraft, could seldom mount a credible air superiority threat. If called upon to contest the control of their airspace against an enemy superior

in numbers, technical quality, and training, they would probably suffer catastrophic casualties.

Instead, the air force will probably confine itself to hit-and-run ground attack missions. Even these will be risky. Soviet-supplied Iraqi aircraft have poor NAW (Night All-Weather) capability and so the Iraqi air force has traditionally foregone night attacks altogether. If hostilities begin, there will be no time to begin learning that type of mission.

Given the massive allied air superiority, it is probable that many, if not all, Iraqi military airfields would be disabled within the first 24-48 hours of hostilities. It is reasonable to expect that many Iraqi aircraft will have been dispersed to remote fields, or will operate from stretches of paved highway, in the absence of their main air bases. While this will be possible for a while, turnaround time will be slower than for aircraft operating from regular bases and aircraft serviceability will probably drop quickly.

1 medium-range bomber squadron (Tu-16)
1 supersonic bomber squadron (Tu-22)
17 ground attack squadrons (MiG-27, Su-7, Su-20, Su-25, Mirage)
16 fighter squadrons (MiG-21, MiG-23, MiG-25, MiG-29, Mirage)

Total of 550 combat aircraft, of which only 150 are modern designs

THE ALLIED FLEETS
SEA POWER

Among the first forces to respond to the crisis in the Persian Gulf were the elements of the U.S. Navy on station in and near the Indian Ocean. These ships were used to support early landings of Marines in Saudi Arabia and to enforce the embargo against Iraq. A number of Allied nations quickly dispatched warships to the area to assist in enforcing the blockade.

As naval strength in the region has grown, increasing attention has been paid to the manner in which naval forces can assist conventional ground operations. Control of the sea lanes is a critical mission, especially when the Allied forces are operating at the end of a long seaborne supply route. Given the relative balance of naval forces in the Gulf, however, the Allied navies seem completely capable of meeting that challenge.

Beyond sea control, navies can exert a direct effect on land and air battles by three means: naval gunfire, naval missile fire, and air power.

NAVAL GUNFIRE

Naval gunfire is the navy's traditional means of supporting land forces. Most modern ships, however, rely on sophisticated anti-ship missile systems, and these systems are generally too expensive to waste pounding ground forces. Most naval vessels have only small, short range gun systems.

The U.S. Navy, however, maintains several big *Iowa*-class battleships, refurbished to carry naval cruise missiles. But they retain their nine 16-inch guns for shore bombardment. These weapons would be ideal for supporting ground actions almost anywhere in Kuwait.

NAVAL MISSILES

The warheads of most naval missiles are too small to be effective against ground targets; the Tomahawk is an exception. These long-range cruise missiles have large warheads and are capable of pinpoint accuracy. Many U.S. naval vessels (including the two battleships in the area) carry them. Many ships deployed to the Gulf are carrying much higher than normal loads.

The powerful *Aegis* cruisers (that form the core of any carrier battle group's escort) are highly capable air defense cruisers with very sophisticated radars. The overwhelming air superiority enjoyed by the allies in the Gulf, however, brings into question how useful their large SAM armament will be. As a result, they now carry twice their normal Tomahawk load at the expense of SAMs. *Aegis* cruisers normally carry 12 Tomahawks and 110 Standard SAMs. Those deployed to the Gulf have between 24 and 48 Tomahawks each, while USS *San Jacinto* has been designated a *special weapons platform* and carries about 100 Tomahawks.

There are usually between six and eight U.S. nuclear submarines in the region, carrying 100 Tomahawks between them.

In all, the Navy has between 300 and 500 Tomahawk Land-Attack Cruise Missiles around Iraq. This tremendous concentration of cruise missiles provides the navy with the ability to make a large number of precision strikes on strategic Iraqi targets, such as airfields, munitions facilities, command control complexes, and so on. The Iraqis have effectively no means of shooting down or deflecting these missiles.

NAVAL AIR POWER

Each U.S. attack carrier has a powerful air group of about 74 planes. Each includes:
24 F-14A Tomcat (fighter)
24 F/A-18 Hornet (fighter/attack)
10 A-6E Intruder (long range attack)
8 S-3A Viking (anti-submarine)
4 EA-6B Prowler (electronic warfare aircraft)
4 E-2C Hawkeye (airborne early warning aircraft)

The Tomcat is one of the most sophisticated and effective air superiority aircraft in the world.

The Hornet can be either an attack aircraft or an agile fighter. Normally, it flies attack missions while Tomcats fly top cover.

Intruders are long-range fighter-bombers. Special fuel tanks make them into tankers allowing combat air patrol (CAP) to stay up longer, or strike missions to fly farther.

Vikings are ASW platforms of little use in the Gulf. However, they are also strike aircraft and carry bombs.

Prowlers use electronic systems to locate and jam enemy radars.

Hawkeyes use their powerful long range radar to track any incoming aircraft, alert the carrier, and direct fighters to the intruders. Half a dozen Hawkeyes gave the Israeli Air Force a decisive edge over the Syrians in Lebanon. U.S. carriers will deploy over twenty of them.

Carrier aircraft bring their airfields with them. Deployment of Allied aircraft to Saudi Arabia and the Gulf states has filled every useable airfield to capacity, and additional air reinforcement virtually has to be by means of carriers. Also, it is much more difficult to hit a carrier than a land base because of its mobility.

NAVAL ORDER OF BATTLE

United States Navy
The Western Mediterranean:
Carrier Group Saratoga
  Attack Carrier (CV): *Saratoga*
  Aegis Cruiser (CGA):
    Philippine Sea (24+ TH)
  Destroyers: *Sampson,*
    Spruance (TH)
  Frigates: *Montgomery, Hart*

Carrier Group Kennedy
  Attack Carrier (CV): *Kennedy*
  Aegis Cruisers (CGA):
    Gates (24+ TH),
    San Jacinto (100+ TH)
  Missile Cruiser (CG):
    Mississippi (TH)
  Destroyer: *Moosbrugger*
  Frigate: *Roberts*
  Supply Ships: *Seattle, Sylvania*

Arabian Sea (Includes
Persian Gulf and Red Sea):
Persian Gulf Squadron
  Command Ships:
    Blue Ridge, LaSalle
  Battleships (BBG):
    Missouri (TH)
    Wisconsin(TH)
  Missile Cruiser: *England (TH)*
  Destroyer: *David Ray*
  Frigates: *Bradley, Reid, Barbey,*
    Vandergrift, Taylor, Rentz
  Minesweepers: *Adroit, Leader,*
    Avenger, Impervious

Persian Gulf Amphibious Group
  Helicopter Carrier: *Inchon*
  Transport: *Nashville*
  Dock Landing Ship:
    Whidbey Island
  Tank Landing Ships:
    Newport, Fairfax County
  Amphibious Ready Group III
    (with 5th Marine Brigade)

Carrier Group Midway
  Attack Carrier (CV): *Midway*
  Aegis Cruisers (CGA):
    Bunker Hill (24+ TH),
    Mobile Bay (24+ TH)
  Destroyers: *Hewitt, Oldendorf*
  Frigates: *Curts, Rodney Davis*

Carrier Group Roosevelt
  Nuclear Carrier (CVN):
    Theodore Roosevelt
  Aegis Cruisers (CGA):
    Leyte Gulf (24+ TH)
  Missile Cruiser (CG):
    Richard K. Turner
  Destroyers: *Caron (60 TH)*
  Frigates: *Hawes, Vreeland*
  Fleet Oiler: *Platte*
  Ammunition Ship: *Santa Barbara*

Carrier Group America
  Attack Carrier (CV): *America*
  Aegis Cruiser (CGA):
    Normandy (26+ TH)
  Missile Cruiser (CG):
    Virginia (8 TH)
  Destroyers:
    Preeble, William V. Pratt
  Frigate: *Haklyburton*
  Fleet Oiler: *Kalamazoo*
  Ammunition Ship: *Nitro*

Carrier Group Ranger
  Attack Carrier (CV): *Ranger*
  Aegis Cruisers (CGA):
    Valley Forge (24+ TH),
    Princeton (24+ TH)
  Destroyers: *Will, Foster*
  Frigate: *Hammond*
  Ammunition Ship: *Shasta*
  Tanker: *Kansas City*

Royal Navy (UK)
Destroyers: *York, Glouchester*
Frigates: *Jupiter, Battleaxe*
Minehunters: *Cattisock,*
  Hurworth, Atherstone
Tanker: *Orangeleaf*
Hospital Ship: *Argus*

Portugal
Supply ship: *Sao Miguel* to act as
replenishment vessel for British

Canada
Destroyers: *Athabascan, Terra*
Nova
Supply Ship: one

Australia
Destroyer: *Brisbane*
Frigate: *Sydney* (replacing
  Adelaide and *Darwin*)
Supply Ship: *Success*

The Allies
DESERT SHIELD
FACT BOOK

France
Frigates: *Protet, Commandant*
Ducuing, Montcalm, Dupleix
Tanker: *Durance*

Belgium
Frigate: *Wandelaar*
Minesweepers: *Iris, Myosotis*
Support Ship: *Zinnia*

Netherlands
Frigates: *Witte de With, Pieter*
Florisz
Support Ship: *Zuiderkruis*

Italy
Frigates: *Orsa, Libeccio, Zeffro*
Corvettes: *Sfinge, Minerva*
Supply Ship: *Stromboli*

Spain
Frigate: *Numancia* (replacing
Santa Maria)
Corvettes: *Diana, Infanta*
Cristina (replacing *Cazadora* and
Descubierta)

Greece
Frigate: *Elli* (replacing *Limnos*)

TH indicates the ship carries
Tomahawk Land Attack Cruise
Missiles.

STRUCTURE OF THE US ARMY

In 1939 the German Army invaded Poland and, despite heroic resistance by the Polish Army, quickly overran the country. However, during the course of the campaign they discovered a fantastic number of problems in their equipment and mobilization procedure. Units trained with one weapon were actually equipped with a different one when called up. Some small arms weapons were extremely dangerous. (German infantry suffered more small arms wounds from their own submachineguns than they did from Polish rifles.)

It has always seemed to this author that if any army in recent memory should have been ready for war, it would have been the Germans in World War II. That they weren't only serves to illustrate that no army is ever completely ready for war when it comes. The test of a really good army is how well it is able to improvise in the critical early months while it is shaking down. By that standard, the US Army has done very well indeed.

The US Army today, despite many nagging problems, is probably the best peacetime army in US history. It is certainly the best-equipped. But beyond considerations of equipment, it is also a very well-trained, well-lead force. Officers and enlisted men and women are very professional and combat units are tough and aggressive.

In one respect, the best armies in the world never fight, because if an army is good enough it never has to. No one is interested in taking them on. If the current crisis in the Gulf is resolved peacefully, it will be due in large measure to the tremendously intimidating combat potential of the US Army.

TOTAL ARMY

The United States Army consists of three principal components:
  the Regular Army,
  the US Army Reserve, and
  the National Guard.

All three elements were closely integrated in a force structure known as the Total Army. Most divisions in the US, for example, had only two Regular Army brigades, and in the event of a crisis they would receive a National Guard brigade. These National Guard "Roundout" brigades were kept at a very high state of combat readiness. By the same token, Regular Army units relied extensively on logistical support units in the reserve structure to sustain them in the event of a protracted operation, such as Desert Shield.

One apparent casualty of the Desert Shield deployment has been the Total Army concept itself. Because there has been a high emphasis placed on immediate deployability, reserve component units have been encouraged to keep a high "fill rate" in their ranks and make sure that all key MOS slots (military occupational specialties) were filled. In many units this was done by deliberately keeping discipline relaxed and retaining key specialists long after they should have been released on medical grounds. One company, for example, immediately after mobilization had to send half a dozen specialists back home. All were over 50 years of age and several had heart conditions.

TACTICAL ORGANIZATION

U.S. heavy divisions (armored and mechanized) are organized along very similar lines. Each division has ten maneuver battalions in its line brigades plus 1 divisional cavalry (mechanized recon) battalion, three artillery battalions, an MLRS battery, one or two helicopter gunship battalions, and a battalion each of engineers and air defense artillery. Armored divisions have six tank battalions and four mechanized battalions, while the proportion is reversed in mechanized divisions. Armored cavalry regiments have three armored cavalry squadrons (battalions), and air cavalry squadron, and an artillery battalion.

Tank battalions consist of a headquarters company and four tank companies. Each tank company has three platoons of four tanks each plus two tanks in the headquarters section. The battalion headquarters company has two command tanks, a cavalry platoon with six M3 Bradley Cavalry Fighting Vehicles (CFV, a variant of the M2 IFV), a platoon with six self-propelled heavy mortars, and a variety of support units.

Mechanized battalions are organized along similar lines. The battalion itself consists of a headquarters company, four mechanized infantry companies, and an anti-armor company. The headquarters company is the same as in the tank battalion except that the command section has M2 Bradleys instead of tanks. The infantry companies each have three platoons (three rifle squads, a command group, and four Bradleys each) and a company command group with another Bradley. The anti-armor company has three platoons, each with four M901 Improved TOW Vehicles and an M-113 command track, plus a small company headquarters and another M-113.

Helicopter gunship battalions each have a headquarters company and three attack helicopter companies. The headquarters company has supporting units and a few observation and utility helicopters for command and support work. Each attack helicopter company has an attack helicopter platoon of seven gunships (AH-1 Cobras or AH-64 Apaches) and a scout platoon of four observation helicopters (OH-58 Kiowas).

Armored cavalry squadrons have an unusual mixed organization. Each squadron (battalion) has a headquarters troop (two command tanks and supporting units), three cavalry troops, and a tank company, organized just like that of a tank battalion. Each cavalry troop (company) has two scout platoons of six M3 Bradley CFVs each, two tank platoons of 4 tanks each, a mortar section with two heavy self-propelled mortars, and a headquarters section with an additional tank. This gives an armored cavalry squadron a total of 43 main battle tanks and 36 CFVs, a very powerful mechanized force.

Artillery battalions consist of three firing batteries, each with two platoons of four guns each, for a total of 24 guns per battalions.

THE PATCHWORK QUILT

The crisis in the Persian Gulf caught the United States Army in a period of transition, and that has caused a number of problems in terms of deployability of units. The fact that we have put as many combat-capable troops in the Gulf as we have is a tribute to the flexibility of the command structure as well as the adaptability of the troops. Nevertheless, getting full-strength divisions to the theater of operations has required a bewildering array of cross-attachments and cobbling together of units.

• 2nd Armored Division was scheduled for demobilization due to cuts in the force structure, and one brigade had already stood down.

That left one brigade in Europe and one in the US. Both brigades are in Saudi Arabia serving under different division headquarters.

• 1st Cavalry Division (Armored) has two Regular Army brigades and a National Guard roundout brigade (155th Armored). As the 155th was not considered sufficiently combat-ready, the 1st Cavalry took the 1st "Tiger" Brigade of the 2nd Armored Division instead.

• 1st Mechanized Division had two brigades in the US and a forward-deployed brigade in Europe. As that brigade was scheduled to return to States-side duty, it was cannibalized for equipment and trained personnel by other units staying in Europe. When the crisis broke out, the forward brigade in Germany was not deployable, and so the division is being reinforced with the 3rd Brigade, 2nd Armored Division from Europe.

• 24th Mechanized division has two Regular Army brigades and a National Guard roundout brigade (48th Mechanized). As the 48th was not considered sufficiently combat-ready, the division took the separate 197th Mechanized Infantry Brigade, the Fort Benning Infantry School brigade, instead.

• When it came time to deploy attack helicopter units to the Gulf, the 6th Air Cavalry Combat Brigade (tasked to support the Rapid Deployment Force in the event of just this sort of crisis) was not combat ready. As a result, the 12th Aviation Brigade (a corps asset) and the aviation brigade of the 3rd Armored Division, both from Europe, were deployed instead.

• The 9th Infantry Division was in the process of switching from a light motorized division to a mechanized division. All of its heavy equipment and most of the personnel trained in its use have been stripped off and fed into departing units to bring them

The Allies

DESERT SHIELD

FACT BOOK

up to strength. The remnants have been reorganized as the 199th Separate Motorized Brigade.

• The 194th Separate Armored Brigade (the Fort Knox Armor School brigade) has been disbanded. Most of its personnel and equipment were fed into departing units to bring them up to strength. What is left has been reorganized as the 10th Cavalry Task Force (a reinforced battalion).

US Army
Total Strength
World Wide

Regular Army: 750,000 men and women

Army National Guard: 587,000 men and women

Army Reserve: 610,000 men and women

18 regular army divisions (4 armored, 7 mechanized, 1 infantry, 4 light infantry, 1 air assault, 1 airborne), 14 separate maneuver brigades and regiments

10 National Guard divisions (2 armored, 2 mechanized, 5 infantry, 1 light infantry), 2 separate maneuver brigades

12 Army Reserve training divisions, 3 separate maneuver brigades.

Tanks: 16,000
IFVs: 5000
APCs: 26,000
Guns: 5400
Armed Helicopters: 2250

FROM MANY, ONE
THE ALLIED ARMIES

A number of nations have sent ground combat troops to Saudi Arabia. The scope of this book does not allow a detailed treatment of these armies, but the brief information and commentary presented below may help the reader understand their capabilities. For a complete listing of Allied ground units in the theater see the Allied Order of Battle.

In most cases below only a part of the country's army is deployed in the Gulf, and so the equipment notes are limited solely to deployed equipment. For example, Egypt continues to operate a large amount of Soviet equipment, but the divisions sent to Saudi Arabia are equipped with tanks and APCs solely of US manufacture.

SA-342K Gazelle (United Arab Emirates)

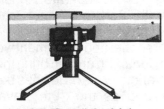

HOT (Saudi Arabia)

84mm Carl Gustav (Qatar)

SAUDI ARABIA
Main Battle Tank
   AMX-30, M-60A3
Armored Recon Vehicle:
   AML-90
Infantry Fighting Vehicle:
   AMX-10P
Armored Personnel Carrier:
   M-113
   V-150 with National Guard
Light Antitank Weapon:
   84mm Carl Gustav
ATGM: TOW, Dragon, HOT
Artillery: M-109 SP 155mm,
   FH-70 and M-198 towed 155mm
Air Defense: Stinger, Redeye,
   40mm, Improved HAWK
Strengths: Well-equipped, apparently good leadership at the top, good morale throughout.
Weaknesses: Poor maintenance procedures, no combat experience.
Comments: Might not have been able to stand the shock of an immediate Iraqi attack, but has benefitted from time to prepare for battle.

UNITED ARAB EMIRATES
Main Battle Tank: AMX-30
Armored Recon Vehicle:
   Scorpion, AML-90
Infantry Fighting Vehicle:
   AMX-10P
Armored Personnel Carrier:
   Panhard M-3
Light Anti-tank Weapon:
   84mm Carl Gustav
ATGM: Milan, TOW, HOT
Artillery: F-3 SP 155mm
   ROF light towed 105mm
Air Defense: 20mm, Rapier
   RBS-70
Attack Helicopter:
   SA-342K Gazelle with HOT
Strengths: Good array of modern equipment.
Weaknesses: No combat experience. Unit cohesion questionable.
Comments: Combat units integrated into a brigade-sized force with other Gulf states. 30% of the armed forces consist of foreign mercenaries.

QATAR
Main Battle Tank: AMX-30
Infantry Fighting Vehicle:
   AMX-10P
Armored Personnel Carrier:
   VAB
Light Anti-tank Weapon:
   84mm Carl Gustav
ATGM: Milan, HOT
Artillery: F-3 SP 155mm
   towed 25-pounders
Air Defense: Rapier, Blowpipe
Attack Helicopter:
   SA-342L Gazelle with HOT
Strengths: Well-equipped.
Weaknesses: No combat experience.

M-109A2 SP 155 mm (Bahrain)

TOW (Oman)

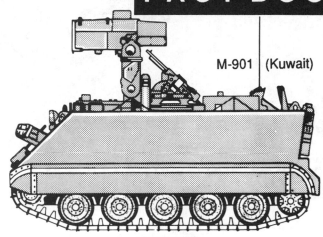

M-901 (Kuwait)

OMAN

Main Battle Tank:
Qayid al-Ardh (Chieftain)
Armored Recon Vehicle:
Scorpion
Armored Personnel Carrier:
Saxon
ATGM: TOW, Milan
Artillery: M-109A2 SP 155mm,
FH-70 towed 155mm
Air Defense: 20mm, 40mm
Blowpipe SAM, Javelin SAM
Rapier SAM
Strengths: Professional army with strong traditions, good training, considerable combat experience versus rebels.
Weaknesses: No experience in large, conventional operations.
Comments: Combat units integrated into a brigade-sized force with other Gulf states. Very pro-West, particularly pro-British.

BAHRAIN

Main Battle Tank: M-60A3
Armored Recon Vehicle:
AML-90
Armored Personnel Carrier
Panhard M-3
ATGM: TOW
Artillery: M-198 towed 155mm
Air Defense: Stinger
Attack Helicopter:
AB-212 Alouette, Bo-105
Comments: Combat units integrated into a brigade-sized force with other Gulf states.

KUWAIT

Main Battle Tank: Chieftain
M84 (Yugoslav-version of T-72)
Armored Recon Vehicle:
Saladin, Ferret
Infantry Fighting Vehicle:
BMP-2
Armored Personnel Carrier:
M-113
Light Anti-tank Weapon:
84mm Carl Gustav
ATGM: HOT
M-901 SP Improved TOW
Artillery: M-109A2 SP 155mm
Air Defense: SA-7
Attack Helicopter:
SA-342K Gazelle with HOT
Strengths: Fighting to recapture homeland. Morale high.
Weaknesses: Numerically weak, little combat experience (until recently), attempting to train and absorb several thousand new recruits.
Comments: Additional M-84s expected from Yugoslavia. Originally had two armored and one mechanized brigade. One of the armored brigades will reform as infantry due to a shortage of tanks.

ZSU-23-4 SP (Syria)

D-30 Towed 122mm (Egypt)

Milan (France)

EGYPT
Main Battle Tank: M-60A3
Armored Recon Vehicle: BRDM-2
Infantry Fighting Vehicle: BMP-1 (may not be present in Saudi Arabia)
Armored Personnel Carrier: M-113
Light Anti-tank Weapon: RPG-7
ATGM: TOW, Milan
Artillery: M-109A2 SP 155mm D-30 towed 122mm
Air Defense: SA-7, SA-9 ZSU-23-4
Attack Helicopter: SA-342L Gazelle with HOT (may not be in Saudi Arabia)
Strengths: Considerable combat experience versus Israel, including large mobile operations. Solid officer and NCO corps. Good training and equipment.
Weaknesses: Unpopularity of cooperation with US among fundamentalist troops causing morale problems.
Comments: A good, solid army.

SYRIA
Main Battle Tank: T-62 (in Saudi Arabia T-55 and T-72 in Syria)
Armored Recon Vehicle: BRDM-2
Infantry Fighting Vehicle: BMP-1
Armored Personnel Carrier: BTR-60
Light Anti-tank Weapon: RPG-7
ATGM: AT-3, AT-4
Artillery: 2S1 SP 122mm 2S3 SP 152mm towed 122mm and 152mm
Air Defense: SA-7, SA-9 SA-13, ZSU-23-4 SP, towed 57mm
Attack Helicopter: Mi-24 Hind, SA-342L Gazelle (in Syria)
Strengths: Considerable combat experience versus the Israelis.
Weaknesses: Uncertain about serving under US command.
Comments: Syria has put aside its difference with the US to participate in the defense effort, because of Saudi influence and if part because of long-standing hostilities between Iraq and Syria.

FRANCE
Main Battle Tank: AMX-30B2
Armored Recon Vehicle: AMX-10RC
Infantry Fighting Vehicle: AMX-10P
Armored Personnel Carrier: VAB
Light Anti-tank Weapon: LRAC F1
ATGM: Milan, HOT
Artillery: TR towed 155mm
Attack Helicopter: SA-342 Gazelle with HOT
Strengths: The light armored division deployed is made up of extremely tough, professional picked troops, including a large number of Foreign Legionnaires. Equipment is good for a mobile, but hard-hitting, mechanized cavalry mission.
Weaknesses: Too lightly equipped to function as an assault division.
Comments: An interesting and useful addition to the Egyptian Corps.

NIGER

One battalion of light infantry deployed. No combat experience or traditions Training and equipment questionable.

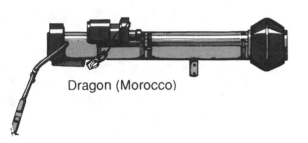

Dragon (Morocco)

BANGLADESH

Little information available

Lynx with TOW (United Kingdom)

The Allies

DESERT SHIELD

FACT BOOK

MOROCCO

Main Battle Tank: M48A5
Armored Personnel Carrier: M-113
Light Anti-tank Weapon: M-79 LAW
ATGM: Dragon, TOW
Artillery: M-109 SP 155mm
Air Defense: SA-7
Strengths: A picked unit. Troops probably have some combat experience fighting Polisario rebels.
Weaknesses: No experience in large-scale conventional operations.

UNITED KINGDOM

Main Battle Tank: Challenger
Armored Recon Vehicle: Scorpion, Scimitar
Infantry Fighting Vehicle: Warrior
Light Anti-tank Weapon: 84mm Carl Gustav
ATGM: Milan, Swingfire
Artillery: M-109A2 SP 155mm
Air Defense: Javelin, Rapier
Attack Helicopter: Lynx with TOW
Strengths: Excellent morale, training, leadership, and traditions. Good equipment.
Comments: No one could ask for better troops to fight alongside.

PAKISTAN

Little information available.
Troop commitment is not popular at home as it is seen as weakening Pakistan's military posture at a time of extremely high tension with India over Kashmir.

CANADA

Main Battle Tank: Leopard 1
Armored Recon Vehicle: M113C and M113R
Armored Personnel Carrier: M113
Light Anti-tank Weapon: Carl Gustav
ATGM: TOW
Artillery: M109
Strengths: Excellent morale, training and leadership.
Comments: 3rd Canadian Mechanized Brigade is one of the best brigades in NATO.

MAIN BATTLE TANK
M1 ABRAMS

The M1 first entered production a decade ago amid some controversy as to its cost and serviceability. With the passage of time these concerns have faded, and the Abrams has proven to be one of the most reliable and cost-effective tanks in the world, and is arguably the best tank available to any army anywhere.

What makes the M1 such an impressive vehicle is the manner in which it has managed to beat the traditional trade-off between armor, firepower, and mobility.

ARMOR

The Abrams was the first tank in the world to incorporate Chobham armor, which is a unique blend of ceramic blocks in a resin matrix sandwiched between sheets of conventional armor plate. This armor is very effective against conventional tank guns, but is extraordinarily so against HEAT rounds, which arm most infantry-carried anti-tank rockets and anti-tank guided missiles. As a result, the basic M1 tank has the equivalent of roughly 350mm of frontal armor protection against conventional guns, but resists HEAT warheads as if it were 750mm thick!

A total of 2374 examples of the basic M1 Abrams were produced from 1980 through 1984. At that time the production lines switched over to producing the IPM1 (Improved Performance M1). A number of minor improvements were incorporated in this version, the most significant of which was the thickening of the turret front armor to make it closer to the effective thickness of the *glacis*, the sloping front of the tank chassis. A total of 894 examples of the IPM1 were produced through 1986. Their frontal armor is estimated at being the equivalent of 400mm thick versus conventional rounds and 1000mm (one meter) thick verus HEAT warheads.

The basic M1A1 has the same armor as the IPM1, the main differences being the mounting of the larger 120mm gun and the incorporation of a chemical defense overpressure system. This system relies on an air compressor to keep the air pressure in the tank higher than the outside, thus keeping any gas from entering. About 1500 M1A1 tanks were built to this configuration from 1986 to 1988.

In 1988 a dramatic new feature was added to the the the M1A1. A mesh of depleted uranium was added to the ceramic matrix of the Chobham armor to increase its resistance to both conventional and HEAT rounds. Although the weight of the vehicle rose from about 55 to almost 65 tons, protection increased dramati-

The Gas Guzzler

The M1 pays a high price for its great mobility. Its fuel efficiency is about 2-5 gallons per mile. Since the M1 carries more fuel onboard than most tanks, its actual radius of action is not much different than any other. However, it will get there quicker and need refueling quicker than most other vehicles. Since it needs to be refueled more often, and needs a fair amount of fuel each time it is topped off, M1 units require a large number of tank trucks, and there is concern whether there are enough deployed with the units. This may limit the speed of any advance, with spearheads required to hold periodically and let their supply columns catch up.

A partial solution is fuel bladders. These are large flexible plastic bags full of fuel carried on the tank itself. The tank doesn't go into combat with them, but instead uses them to top off just before action. To do so the crew pushes the bladder off the tank onto the ground, connects the bladder's hose to the fuel tank, and then drives the tank slowly over the bladder. As the tank flattens the bladder, the fuel is forced up the hose into the tank. Although the Marines have taken a large number of fuel bladders to Saudi Arabia with their tank units, the Army apparently had few on hand when the crisis broke.

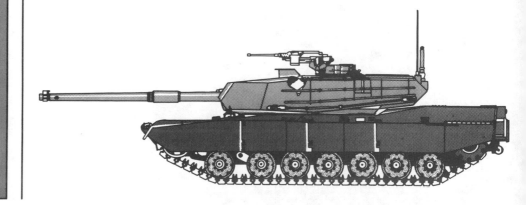

cally. This improved version of the M1A1 has frontal armor which provides protection equivalent to 600mm of hardened steel versus conventional rounds and over 1300mm versus HEAT rounds, making it the best protected tank in the world by a considerable margin.

About 2700 M1A1 tanks have been built with depleted uranium armor, making this the single most numerous variant of the Abrams. The majority of the M1A1 tanks deployed to Saudi Arabia are probably of this type.

FIREPOWER

By use of a sophisticated fire control system, excellent gun stabilization, and advanced ammunition, its firepower is second to none. Its predecessor, the M60A1, had a 50% chance of hitting a tank-sized target at 1500 meters while it (the firing tank) was stationary. The M1 can do better than that at 2000 meters while moving cross-country at 30 kilometers per hour. Of equal importance, the integrated gunsight and ballistic computer of the M1 is easier for the gunner to operate than more primitive gunsights, which often require multiple steps in the aiming process and some mental calculation by the gunner.

The basic M1 mounts the British-designed L7 105mm gun, which remains a very capable system when using the ultra-modern, depleted uranium-tipped ammunition currently available. However, to increase its ability to deal with future threats, the M1A1 was introduced mounting the German-designed 120mm smoothbore cannon. Although a few tankers are unhappy with this variant because it carries fewer main gun rounds (40 in the M1A1 as opposed to 55 in the M1), there is no question that the gun can master any tank encountered on the modern battlefield.

MOBILITY

The field in which the M1 has surged ahead of other tanks most dramatically has been mobility. The M1 is extraordinarily fast, and its suspension gives it a very smooth cross-country ride. One M1 tank platoon commander described its ride at high speed as being like a surfboard. Its road speed is 72 kilometers per hour (45 miles per hour), and its cross-country speed is virtually the same.

It can sustain this sort of speed cross-country due not only to its suspension, but also to its powerful engine which gives it high acceleration and a solid reserve of power to draw on. In rolling country most observers can see tanks coming, even if the tanks are hidden by the rolling ground, because of the clouds of diesel smoke. When you're out driving on the highway, notice how large trucks have to downshift when going uphill, and when they do so their engines strain and release diesel smoke. Tanks behave exactly the same way, except for the M1. Its gas turbine has sufficient power reserves, even at high speed, that it takes hills with virtually no loss in speed and no telltale exhaust plume.

The Allies
DESERT SHIELD
FACT BOOK

	Equivalent to mm of hard steel	Added effect against HEAT
M1A1 with DU Armor	600 mm	1300 mm versus HEAT
M1A1, IPM 1	400 mm	1000 mm versus HEAT
M1	350 mm	750 mm versus HEAT
T-55	200 mm	versus all ammunitions

TANK ARMOR

WORKHORSES AND CHARGERS
ALLIED AFVS

Armored Fighting Vehicles (AFVs) are the mainstays of modern armies. An AFV is not necessarily a tank: it can be a personnel carrier, an armored scout car, or an infantry fighting vehicle.

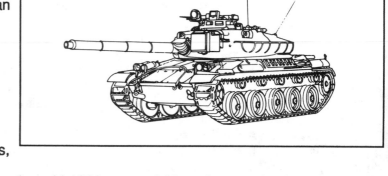

AMX-30 MBT
Weight: 36 tons
Speed: 65 k/h
Gun: 105mm, coincidence RF
Ammo: 47
Armor: 150mm
In Use With: Saudi Arabia, United Arab Emirates, Qatar

Comments: The AMX-30, produced by France from the mid-1960s, was designed to emphasize speed and firepower over armor protection. For maximum protection, it adopted a 105mm gun optimized to fire HEAT rounds, as those were the best armor penetrators at that time. The passage of time has proven most of the AMX-30's design decisions to be wrong. Chobham and reactive armor have significantly reduced the value of HEAT warheads. New hyper-velocity rounds are excellent penetrators, but the AMX-30's gun is not powerful enough to take full advantage of them. New power plant technology has increased the speed of most tanks to equal or better than that of the AMX-30. This leaves it a lightly armored tank of average speed and mediocre killing power.

CHIEFTAIN MK 5 MBT
Weight: 55 tons
Speed: 48 k/h
Gun: 120mm
Armor: 400mm
In Use With: Oman, Kuwait.

Comments: When introduced the Chieftain had the thickest armor and most powerful gun of any tank in the world. It was also extremely slow, although the current production versions are better in that regard.

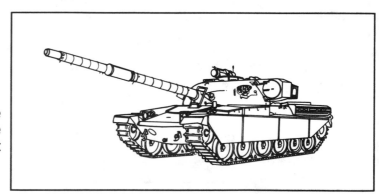

CHALLENGER MBT
Weight: 62 tons
Speed: 60 k/h
Gun: 120mm
Ammo: 52
In Use With: United Kingdom
Armor: 500mm (800mm versus HEAT warheads)

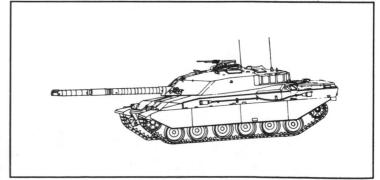

Comment: The Challenger has been a considerable disappointment in service due to problems with the main gun. The Challenger uses a modified version of the Chieftain's rifled 120mm gun which allows it to fire new hyper-velocity APFSDS ammunition. However the new gun is much less accurate than both the Chieftain's rifles 120mm and the M1A1's 120mm smoothbore.

M48A5 MBT
  Weight: 49 tons
  Speed: 48.2 k/h
  Gun: 105mm
  Ammo: 54
  Armor: 250mm
  In Use With: Morocco
  Comment: The progressive upgrades of the M-48 demonstrate the soundness of the basic design. The M-48A5 is nearly as capable as the M-60A3, but has active infrared vision instead of the more effective thermal sight.

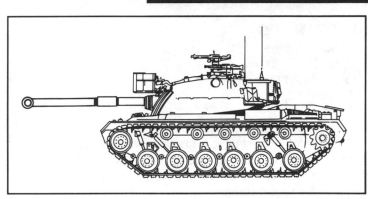

M60A3 MBT
  Weight: 51.5 tons
  Speed: 48.28 k/h
  Gun: 105mm
  Ammo: 63
  Armor: 250mm
  In Use With: Saudi Arabia, Bahrain, Egypt, USMC
  Comments: USMC M-60s are equipped with reactive armor blocks which provides additional protection against HEAT warheads. There are about 50 marine M-60A3s with the 1st Brigade, 50 with the 7th Brigade, and about 20 with the 4th Brigade.

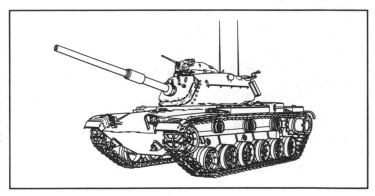

M113 APC
  Weight: 11.16 tons
  Road Speed: 67.6 k/h
  CC Speed:
  Gun: 12.7mm
  Troops: 11
  Armor: 30mm.
  In Use With: Saudi Arabia, Kuwait, Egypt, Morocco
  Comments: One of the most widely used armored vehicles in history. Egyptian M-113s have applique armor which increases the protection to between 50 and 60mm.

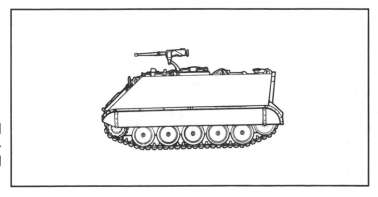

M2 BRADLEY IFV

Weight: 22.59 tons
Speed: 66 k/h
Gun: 25mm + TOW
Troops: 7
Armor: 30mm (M2), 60mm (M2A1)
In Use With: US Army

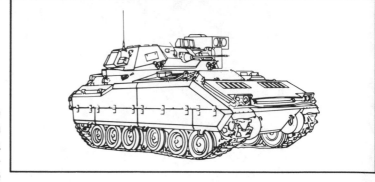

Comments: The Bradley's side armor consists of two 1/4-inch hard steel plates and an offset 1-inch aluminum plate. The space between the plates provides extra protection against spaced charges. Overall the equivalent protection against conventional rounds is the same as 30mm of steel. The later variant (M2A1) has 30mm of steel applique armor added to the front and sides. Most vehicles with VII Corps are of the improved type.

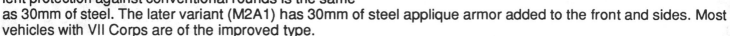

SPARTAN APC

Weight: 8 tons
Speed: 80 k/h
Gun: 7.62mm
Troops: 4
Armor: 20mm
In Use With: United Kingdom

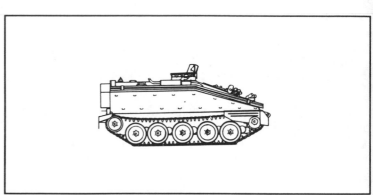

Comments: Spartan is a small, light APC built on the same chassis as the Scorpion and Scimitar and designed to work with them. It has been widely exported as an APC for recon units.

AMX-10P IFV

Weight: 14.2 tons
Speed: 65 k/h
Gun: 20mm
Troops: 8
Armor: 30mm
In Use With: France, Saudi Arabia, United Arab Emirates, Qatar

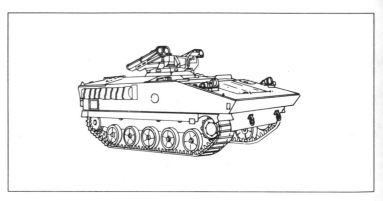

Comment: The turret has a mounting which can accept a Milan missile. Usually the squad has a Milan launcher which it will mount on the vehicle during an advance but will dismount when occupying defensive positions. Some AMX-10Ps in the region are used as SP mounts for HOT ATGM systems. A popular vehicle.

BMP-2 IFV

Weight: 14 tons
Speed: 70 k/h
Gun: 30mm
Missile: AT-4
Ammo: 200 30mm, 3 AT-4 missiles
Troops: 7
Armor: 25-30mm
In Use With: Kuwait

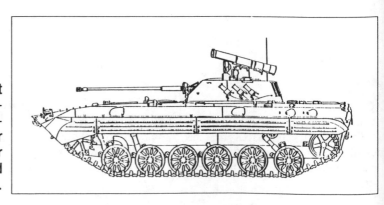

Comment: This is the improved version of the Soviet BMP-1. Principal visual differences include a larger 2-man turret placed farther back on the chassis, a long-barreled autocannon in place of the shorter, thicker 73mm smoothbore, and a tubular missile launcher mounted on a pedestal in the center of the turret instead of an exposed missile on a launch rail over the gun tube.

The Allies
DESERT SHIELD
FACT BOOK

AAV-7A1 ARMORED AMPHIBIOUS TROOP CARRIER
Weight: 23 tons
Speed: 64 kph
Gun: 12.7mm machinegun
Troops: 25
Armor: 30mm+
In Use With: USMC
Comments: Originally designated the LVTP-7, this is a slightly improved version. Over 800 are in service worldwide, and over half of these are in or on their way to the Persian Gulf, enough to lift almost all of the Marine infantry units present.

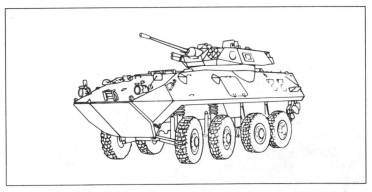

LAV-25 IFV
Weight: 14 tons
Speed: 95 kph
Gun: 25mm
Ammo: 200
Troops: 6
Armor: 25mm
In Use With: USMC
Comments: Each USMC division has a light armored assault battalion with over 100 LAV-25s. These are allocated by company to individual marine expeditionary brigades, with each having an average of about 50 vehicles, enough to mechanize a Marine infantry battalion.

M-551 SHERIDAN AIRBORNE LIGHT TANK
Weight: 16 tons
Speed: 65 kph
Gun: 152mm gun/launcher
Ammo: 20 cannon rounds, 10 Shillelagh missiles
Armor: 100mm
In Use With: US 82nd Airborne Division
Comments: Originally intended as a general-purpose reconaissance vehicle, the Sheridan experienced continuous problems with its main armament, which consists of a gun capable of firing either a 152mm low velocity round or a Shillelagh missile. In practice, the recoil generated by firing a conventional round often damages the missile guidance system rendering the launcher inoperative. Because of this and other problems it was phased out of general service, but still equips the airborne light tank battalion of the 82nd Airborne Division, and these were the first US tanks to arrive in Saudi Arabia.

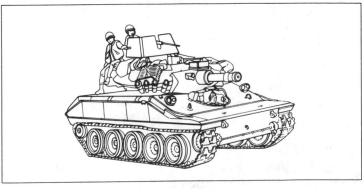

An additional quirk of the Sheridan is that the gun's recoil generates sufficient torque to make the turret slew a few degrees, turning the traverse wheel about an eighth of a turn very suddenly. If the gunner continues to hold the traverse wheel and fires the gun with the floor petal, the sudden turn will usually break his wrist. Experienced Sheridan gunners, of course, know to take their hand away.

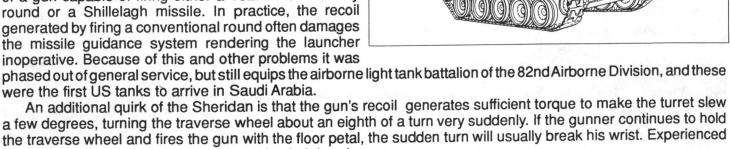

DEVELOPMENT OF OPERATIONS
STRATEGIC OPTIONS

If war comes, what options are open to Allied troops to force Iraq out of Kuwait? Geography and Iraqi deployments provide some general limits within which Allied operations officers will have to work. Within those limits, an offensive plan will probably take one of three forms: Plans A, B, and C.

None of these are official plans announced by the U.S. or Allied armed forces; they are purely speculative, but nonetheless based on solid facts and reasonable assumptions.

THE OPENING MOVES

Regardless of which plan is adopted, the campaign would begin with a massive air and naval bombardment of Iraq. Tactical aircraft (strike aircraft and fighter bombers) will concentrate on Iraqi airbases, surface to air and surface to surface missile sites, identified command posts, supply roads, fuel dumps, ammo dumps, bridges, and highways.

B-52s from Egypt and Diego Garcia, F-111s from Turkey, and navy Tomahawk cruise missiles will concentrate on deeper strategic targets. High priority items will be chemical, biological, and nuclear storage, research, and fabrication facilities, military factories, and national command centers.

These air attacks will start at night and will continue throughout the first day. Air superiority fighters will rotate to keep a constant airborne interceptor force which will be vectored against any Iraqi aircraft by AWACS planes. Artillery will join in as well and begin pounding forward Iraqi troop concentrations along the front. Special Forces teams may be inserted into northern Iraq to help organized Kurdish resistance groups.

Since the Allied forces will not move prior to the expiration of the U.N. resolution deadline, there will be no chance of achieving genuine strategic surprise. Ground troops will, therefore, probably not jump off on the first day, but will rather let the air, naval, and artillery bombardment do its job. Ground forces will probably jump off on D+1.

US POLICY CONSTRAINTS

From a purely military point of view, the clear solution to the problems posed by the Iraqi occupation of Kuwait involve the capture of Baghdad as rapidly as possible. Striking at the industrial, transportation, and political nerve center of the country allows the victor to dictate terms. There are, however, elements of the political equation which make this course of action more difficult.

• There is reasonably strong domestic US support for military action to free Kuwait from Iraqi occupation. Support for a war aimed at toppling Hussein's government, even as a means of securing Kuwaiti independence, is less strong.

• All of the allied units present are willing to fight in defense of Saudi territorial integrity. Many of them, particularly from the Arab world, are less willing to fight an offensive campaign against Iraq. They could still be used to screen less active parts of the front. However, as US units drive deeper into Iraqi territory, these flank guards either must also move in or the spearheads must begin detaching units to guard the flanks.

• A campaign, such as outlined in "Plan C," which involves a major drive on Baghdad and virtually no ground attacks on Kuwait, runs the risk of appearing to be simple aggression against Iraq. If Kuwait is the actual issue, many will ask, why is the Army ignoring it? Isn't the US using the occupation of Kuwait as an excuse for aggression against the government and people of Iraq? The fact that this may be the cheapest way of freeing Kuwait will be lost on many.

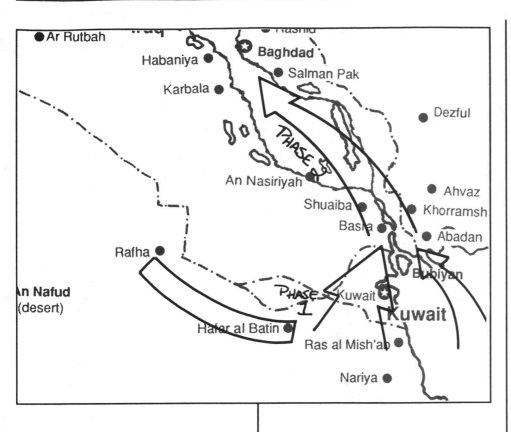

PLAN A

The main body of 3rd Army's attack will follow the axis Nariya-Kuwait City. The Egyptian Corps will sidestep to the left and provide flank security from Rafha to Hafar al Batin, while the Saudi I Corps remains in reserve. U.S. VII and XVIII Corps will drive through the forward Iraqi positions and link up with a combined amphibious and airmobile assault on Kuwait City. Amphibious operations further north are possible as well.

Phase 1 will involve the destruction of the Iraqi III, IV, and VIII Tank Corps in Kuwait. Phase 2 will involve a move on Basra, defeat of the Iraqi armored reserves stationed there, and then a drive up the Tigris-Euphrates valley to Baghdad.

Advantages

+ Land forces remain close to the Persian Gulf for the critical phase of the campaign, allowing them to benefit from flanking amphibious invasions and naval gunfire support.

+ Results in rapid liberation of Kuwait.

+ Uses best supply lines available for the campaign: roads through Kuwait, naval shipping in the Gulf, communication lines up the Tigris and Euphrates.

Disadvantages

- Plays to Iraqi strength; attacks where Iraqis are thickest on the ground and heavily entrenched. What the British call, "Going for the thickest part of the hedge."

- Commits US troops to costly frontal assaults and positional warfare where their advantages in mobility are largely meaningless.

- Requires a long advance up the difficult, swampy country north of Basra.

THE US MARINE CORPS

Active Force: 195,000 men and women

Reserves: 87,000 men and women

3 regular divisions (total of six brigades plus separate battalions)

1 reserve division (3 regiments)

Tanks: 700

IFVs: 400

APCs: 800

Guns: 1000

Armed Helicopters: 80

Combat Aircraft: 490

THE DATING GAME

Of late there has been considerable speculation concerning a possible jumpoff date for an attack on Iraqi forces in Kuwait, assuming that a peaceful settlement is not reached. There are two principal criteria for such an attack date: high tides after midnight at the head of the Gulf (to facilitate a pre-dawn amphibious landing) and low light conditions.

Light is particularly significant, and widely misunderstood. The best time to attack, contrary to some published statements, is not at or before the new moon, as some US night sights require some background light to function at peak efficiency. The best time is several days after the new moon, when there is slightly more ambient light.

Tides are important if an amphibious invasion is to be made. The marines have conducted a number of practice amphibious assaults, and have reported that the Persian Gulf may be the most difficult area in the world in which to conduct such an operation. That being the case, *(Continued next page.)*

THE US NAVY

Active Force: 584,000 men and women

Reserves: 242,000 men and women

Ballistic Missile Submarines: 35

Nuclear Attack Submarines: 93

Attack Carriers: 14

Battleships: 4

Cruisers: 41

Destroyers: 68

Frigates: 102

Light Combatants: 30

Amphibious Ships: 66

Support Vessels: 152

Combat Aircraft: 1580

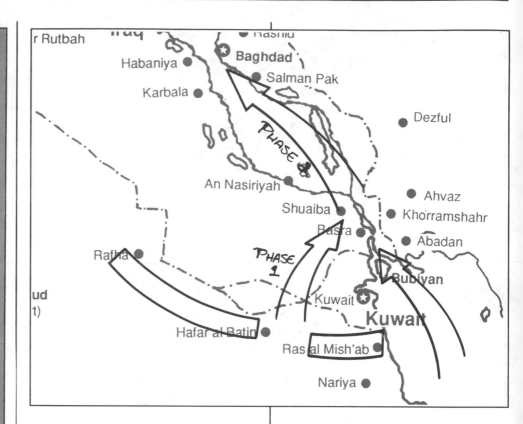

PLAN B

The main body of 3rd Army's attack follows the line of the wadi (dry riverbed) that runs northeast from Hafar al Batin and along the old Iraqi-Kuwaiti border. The Egyptian Corps will sidestep to the left and provide flank security from Rafha to Hafar al Batin, while the Saudi I Corps covers the Saudi-Kuwait border. US VII and XVIII Corps will drive along the rough line of the Wadi toward Basra, outflanking the Iraqi III, IV, and VIII Tank Corps from the northwest. Simultaneously, amphibious and airmobile assaults will be launched near Bubiyan Island to cut off the retreat of Iraqi troops in Kuwait. VII and XVIII Corps will defeat the Iraqi armored reserves near Basra and relieve the beachhead, completing Phase 1, the encirclement of Iraqi forces in Kuwait.

Phase 2 will involve drive up the Tigris-Euphrates valley to Baghdad, while the bulk of Iraqi forces are contained by allied units and disrupted by continuous air attacks.

Advantages

+ Land forces remain close to the Persian Gulf for the critical phase of the campaign, allowing them to benefit from flanking amphibious invasions and naval gunfire support.

+ Outflanks the main Iraqi concentration in Kuwait rather than hitting it head-on.

+ Uses best supply lines available for the later phase of the campaign.

Disadvantages

- Requires an advance through difficult, roadless countryside.

- Relies on everything working according to plan. Nothing ever goes according to plan. An unforeseen setback could leave VII and XVIII Corps halted short of the objective, an isolated Marine and airborne beachhead under heavy Iraqi pressure, and the Iraqis in a central position, able to switch the tanks of 11 heavy divisions to hit each US force in turn.

- If successful, it requires a long advance up the difficult, swampy country north of Basra.

PLAN C

The main body of 3rd Army's attack follows the road from Rafha north to An Najaf, and then to Baghdad. The Egyptian Corps provides flank security from Rafha to Hafar al Batin at first, but quickly moves its left flank forward into Iraq using Hafar al Batin as a pivot of maneuver. The corps provides flank security for the main advance and pins Iraqi mobile reserves in the south. The Saudi I Corps covers the Saudi-Kuwait border and conducts pinning attacks against the Iraqi III and IV Corps. US VII and XVIII Corps drive north while the Marines fake amphibious landings in the Gulf to misdirect the Iraqis as to the actual target of the drive. Airborne and airmobile units move ahead of the advancing armored spearheads and seize critical road junctions before the Iraqis have time to organize their defense. The Allies defeat the main Iraqi reserves, probably built around the II Guards Corps, west of Baghdad.

Advantages

+ Outflanks the main Iraqi concentrations in Kuwait and at Basra rather than hitting them head-on.
+ Clearly focuses on one war-winning objective: Baghdad.
+ Makes maximum use of US operational mobility.

Disadvantages

- Requires that the allies supply an extended campaign through difficult country cut by few roads (and none of them particularly good).
- Does not allow full use of Marine amphibious capability except as a feint in the opening phases.
- Offers Iraqi mobile forces in southern Iraq and Kuwait the opportunity for a counteroffensive into Saudi Arabia.

The Allies
DESERT SHIELD
FACT BOOK

THE DATING GAME
(Continued.)

they will need all the help they can get from the tides.

January 15 is a new moon. Two days later (January 17) there would be sufficiently light, and for three days there are acceptable tides. The next period when both light and tides are correct is February 15-18.

The problem with the January date is that the 17th is also the start of the Islamic month of Rajab: fighting during this month is considered sinful. Rajab ends on February 14, just in time for the February 15-18 window. The problem with the February window is that it is uncomfortably close to the March sandstorm season.

THE US AIR FORCE

Active Force: 579,000 men and women
Air National Guard: 115,000 men and women
Reserves: 129,000 men and women
25 tactical combat wings
3,200 combat aircraft
21 bomber wings
360 strategic bombers
6 strategic missile wings
1,000 ICBM

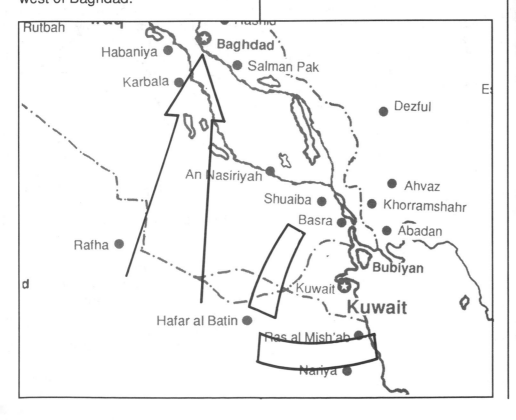

WILD CARDS

Plans A, B, and C cover the most likely course of events should war come to the Arabian Peninsula. In any situation as complex as this one, there are always imponderables—the wild cards. Each of the major countries in the region capable of taking an additional hand in military events is covered very briefly below.

Attempting to predict the actions of any nation in this sort of situation is difficult and almost pointless. That is why military intelligence officers are trained to assess enemy capabilities, rather than try to second-guess their intentions. This section is not meant to *predict* the actions of these countries. Instead it is hoped that it will help the reader better *understand* those actions, or lack of actions as events unfold.

USSR

While the Soviet Union has repeatedly declared that it will not send ground troops to the Gulf, recent exercises by airborne troops near the southern border had caused some speculation that they might be sent to bolster the Allied effort. The possible motive for this would have been to convince the West that the Soviet Union is interested in cooperating in international affairs.

It now appears that the exercises concentrated on crowd control and antiriot tactics, and that the paratroopers are being prepared to deal with the escalating level of internal violence in the Soviet Union. As to convincing the West that the Soviet forces not intended as a threat, every decision-maker who counts is already convinced.

TURKEY

Turkey is Iraq's northern neighbor. Before World War I, Iraq was a province of the Turkish Empire. The increasing influence of the Pan-Turkism political movement in Turkey has brought an increased interest in reasserting Turkish dominance in the region.

The Turkish 2nd Army, headquartered at Malatya, is responsible for guarding the southern border with Iraq and Syria. It is normally 65,000 strong, but by mid-September had been reinforced to 95,000. This probably represents the addition of four separate heavy brigades. The closest source of reinforcements would be from 3rd Army (headquarters Erzurum) which has a total of four heavy brigades in addition to the infantry units necessary to cover the Soviet and Iranian borders. Additional heavy forces could be transferred west from the 1st Army stationed in Istanbul and Thrace.

Due to the crowding of airfields in the Persian Gulf, long-range US F-111 strike aircraft have deployed to Turkish airfields and, in the event of war, will fly missions from there.

Arguments For Intervention: Reassert influence in Middle Eastern affairs. Prove value as an ally to United States and regional powers.

Arguments Against Intervention: No practical invasion route without Syrian cooperation. Long and difficult supply lines if a decisive campaign is to be waged. High cost for no tangible reward.

Probability of Intervention: Fair.

Military Strength
Army: 530,000
Tanks: 3,700
Guns: 2,100
Armed Helicopters: c.20
Combat Aircraft: 360a
Combat Proficiency: High

ISRAEL

Although relations between Israel and the Arab states have always been stormy, to say the least, there is particular bitterness between Israel and Iraq. This was most recently illustrated by the Israeli Air Force's destruction of the Iraqi nuclear power plant capable of making weapons-grade plutonium. Of all the Arab states, Iraq is the only one which did not agree to an armistice with Israel at the end of the Israeli War of Independence in the late-40s, nor have they agreed to any subsequent armistices. Consequently, Israel and Iraq have technically and legally been in a continuous state of warfare for 42 years.

One very real possibility is that Israel might become drawn into hostilities by an Iraqi long-range attack on population centers, either with chemical weapons or conventional warheads on long-range missiles. Iraq might do this in the hopes that active Israeli operations against Iraq would splinter the Arab alliance. If Israeli Air Force units made frequent overflights of Jordanian airspace it might draw Jordan into the conflict as well.

Arguments For Intervention: Traditional animosity toward Iraq. Preemptive strike against perceived chemical, nuclear, or biological threat. Retaliation in the event of an actual Iraqi air or missile attack.

Arguments Against Intervention: Catastrophic impact on cohesion of Gulf Alliance would work to Iraq's benefit. No means of employing land forces. Air forces would have to overfly Syria or Jordan repeatedly.

Probability of Intervention: Voluntarily—Nil. Involuntarily—Fair.

Military Strength
Army: 100,000 (quickly up to 600,000 upon mobilization)
Tanks: 3,800
Guns: 1,400
Armed Helicopters: 75
Combat Aircraft: 575
Combat Proficiency: Outstanding

JORDAN

Of all the participants in the Gulf crisis, Jordan's position is nearly the most difficult. While the economic blockade of Iraq was only an inconvenience for the majority of nations, it was an economic catastrophe for Jordan, for two reasons. First, Jordan relies heavily on tourism for hard currency, and the tourist trade is effectively gone pending resolution of the crisis. Second, Jordan only significant trading partner is Iraq. Most imports to Jordan are good for transshipment to Iraq, and Iraq is Jordan's major supplier of oil. Promised economic assistance from the Saudis has been slow to materialize and Jordan's economy is on the brink of collapse.

Arguments For Intervention: Vital economic links to Iraq. Recent history of military cooperation. (Iranian Chieftains captured by Iraq were turned over to Jordan and added to their armored units.)

Arguments Against Intervention: Low probability of success. Catastrophic long-term results from failure. Moderate, responsible leadership not prone to reckless adventurism.

Probability of Intervention: Low.

Military Strength
Army: 74,000
Tanks: 1,100
Guns: 250
Armed Helicopters: 24
Combat Aircraft: 100
Combat Proficiency: Very High.

SYRIA

Syria and Iraq have long-standing differences. Although Syria did not become involved in the Iran-Iraq war, it was openly sympathetic to Iran. If Syria were to open a "second front" against northwestern Iraq after hostilities began, it would allow Syrian troops to participate in the war other than under US command.

Arguments For Intervention: Traditional differences with Iraq and animosity toward Saddam Hussein. Participation in allied effort separate from US command.

Arguments Against Intervention: Poor road net in northwest of Iraq makes supply difficult. Other Arab states would perceive move as a "stab in the back".

Probability of Intervention: Fair.

Military Strength
Army: 300,000
Tanks: 4,000
Guns: 2,100
Armed Helicopters: 110
Combat Aircraft: 500
Combat Proficiency: Fair.

The Allies
DESERT SHIELD
FACT BOOK

IRAN

Iran is Iraq's neighbor to the east and they have just concluded a long and costly war. In order to free troops from his eastern flank, Saddam Hussein recently ceded all territory Iraq captured during the war back to Iran.

Arguments For Intervention: Traditional animosity toward Iraq.

Arguments Against Intervention: Unwillingness to cooperate with or assist US. Lack of tangible war aims. Low current level of combat readiness.

Probability of Intervention: Low

Military Strength
Army: 300,000 plus 250,000 Revolutionary Guards (*Pasdaran*)
Tanks: 500
Guns: 800
Armed Helicopters: 100
Combat Aircraft: 120 (70 serviceable)
Combat Proficiency: Fair to Poor.

IRAQ
THE ADVERSARY

VITAL STATISTICS
Pop: 17,800,000
GNP: $45 billion
GNP growth: –4%
Inflation: 22%
Debt: $80 billion

Men of Military Age
13-17:   1,071,000
18-22:   873,000
23-32:   1,313,000
Total: 3,257,000

Armed Forces
Active: 1,200,000
Reserve: 650,000
Total: 1,850,000

SADDAM HUSSEIN

Saddam Husayn 'Abd-al-Majid al-Tikriti (better known by the anglicized spelling of his name, Hussein) was born in 1935 or 1937 (sources differ) in the Iraqi province of Tikrit (as his name indicates). He took a degree in law from Baghdad University in 1971, but had been active in Iraqi politics since he joined the Ba'ath (Renaissance) Socialist Party (BPI) in 1956. He participated in an attempted coup in 1959, and was imprisoned from 1964 to 1966, when he escaped. When the BPI ascended to power in 1968, Hussein occupied a number of offices within the party and the government, eventually becoming president of the republic of Iraq and Chairman of the Revolutionary Council of the BPI in 1979, posts which he still holds.

Hussein has acquired an international reputation for ruthlessness and brutality during his undeclared war against the Kurds (an ethnic group in Iran comprising about 1/5th of the population in 1979) and during his war with Iran from 1980 to 1988.

The Iraqi Army has recently ended a war with Iran that has gone on for nearly a decade. While the war was costly for both sides. The Iranian and Iraqi armies emerged with distinctly different battlefield doctrines and combat reputations.

As the war progressed, the Iranian Army relied increasingly on massed infantry attacks, dramatically – but accurately – described in the news media as "human wave assaults." Losses were high, and offensives were preceded by highly publicized massing of new young volunteer battalions for the front. Most of these attacks collapsed in the face of ghastly casualties.

The Iraqis, who had only one third the population base of Iran (18 million versus 54 million), could not afford to suffer the same rates of casualties, and so became masters of entrenchments, camouflage, and above all, flexible use of mobile reserves. Their armaments industry developed innovative means of increasing imported weapon systems, and in the face of the arms blockade learned to manufacture their own munitions, from small arms to theater missiles. Mechanized units became well-practiced at the art of fast-moving and hard-hitting counterattacks to shatter infantry penetrations. Air Force pilots showed a willingness by the end of the war to press attacks on ground targets in the face of Navy anti-aircraft fire.

The resulting army is one which, even if badly overmatched by their adversaries, will give a tough account of itself. If diplomacy fails and war comes to the Persian Gulf, no victory will be gained cheaply, and no prudent man or woman should think that victory is necessarily a foregone conclusion.

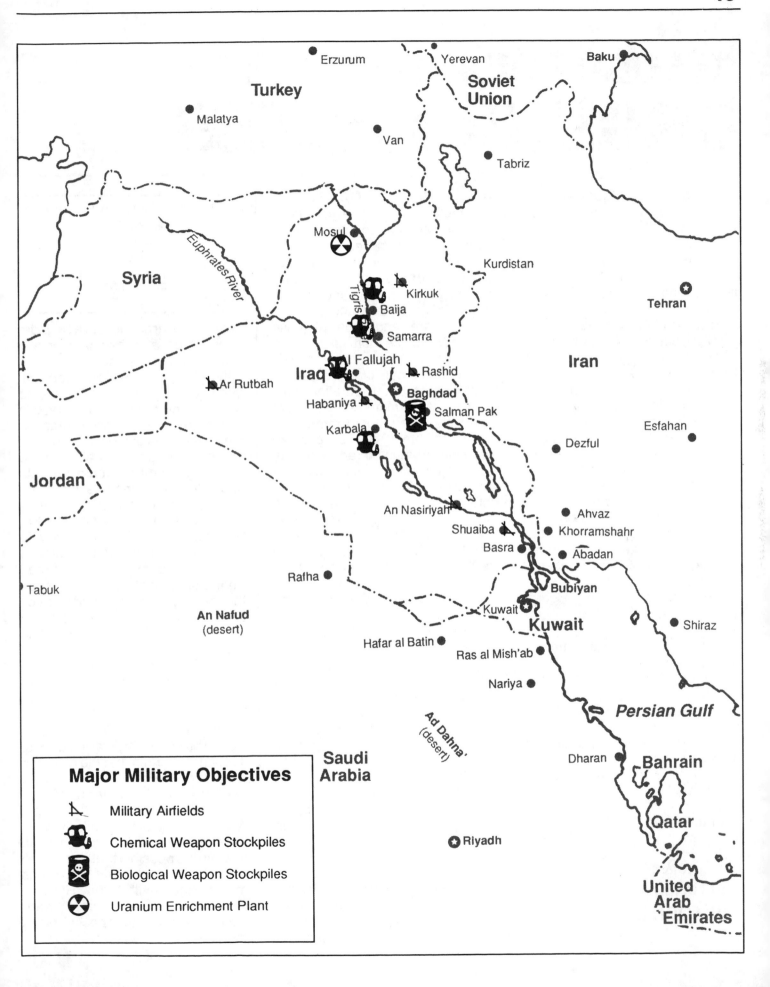

Erzurum

Yerevan

Baku

Turkey

Soviet Union

Malatya

Van

Tabriz

Euphrates River

Mosul

Syria

Kurdistan

Tigris

Kirkuk

Baija

Tehran

Samarra

Iraq

Al Fallujah

Rashid

Iran

Ar Rutbah

Baghdad

Habaniya

Salman Pak

Esfahan

Karbala

Dezful

Jordan

An Nasiriyah

Ahvaz

Shuaiba

Khorramshahr

Basra

Abadan

Tabuk

Rafha

Bubiyan

An Nafud
(desert)

Kuwait

Kuwait

Shiraz

Hafar al Batin

Ras al Mish'ab

Nariya

Persian Gulf

Ad Dahna'
(desert)

Dharan

Bahrain

Saudi Arabia

Qatar

Major Military Objectives

Military Airfields

Chemical Weapon Stockpiles

Biological Weapon Stockpiles

Uranium Enrichment Plant

Riyadh

United Arab Emirates

IRAQI ORDER OF BATTLE
GROUND FORCES

Controlling Headquarters

7 regular corps headquarters (numbered I-VII)

3 reserve corps headquarters (VIII Tank, IX Reserve, X Reserve)

2 Presidential Guard corps headquarters (I Guard, II Guard)

Units and Formations

17 regular infantry divisions

10 regular motorized infantry divisions

14 reserve infantry divisions (mobilized since August 1, 1990, some with only two brigades)

6 regular armored divisions

1 reserve armored division (mobilized since August 1, 1990)

3 mechanized divisions

1 naval infantry division

6 special forces divisions

1 air assault brigade

22 separate infantry brigades

1 or 2 special forces brigades per corps

1 or 2 artillery brigades per corps

2 Presidential Guard tank divisions

1 Presidential Guard mechanized division

1 Presidential Guard motorized division

3 Presidential Guard infantry division

1 Presidential Guard special forces division

2 Surface to Surface Missile Brigades

Total Strength: 1,200,000 men

IRAQI SPECIAL FORCES

In the United States Army, and in most armies for that matter, the term "special forces" implies an irregular or commando-type mission. U.S. special forces, for example, specialize in training indigenous troops in light infantry and guerrilla-type warfare, and excel at those sorts of missions themselves.

Iraqi special forces are completely different. The bulk of Iraq's army is infantry, but the concentration of the best troops in armored, mechanized, and Republican Guard formations left the infantry divisions incapable of mounting much of an offensive. To maximize the effectiveness of what quality troops were left to the infantry, divisions began forming special forces companies during the war with Iran. The closest historical parallel to these companies would be the German *Stosstruppen* of late World War I.

In that conflict, Germany also faced the problem of coaxing offensive operations out of depleted and battle-weary infantry formations, and did so by concentrating the very best troops of a division in its *Stosskompanie*. Each of these companies received additional training and was given extra weapons to carry out its mission, which was to spearhead the division's attack.

The Iraqi special forces companies are nearly identical in concept. They are the best troops in the division and receive the best weapons. If the division has any APCs, they are usually given to the special forces detachment. By the end of the war with Iran most divisions had a full special forces battalion and a few divisions had

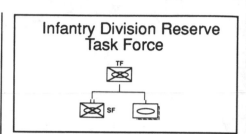

Infantry Division Reserve Task Force

two or three grouped into a brigade. Each corps also has one or two special forces brigades.

In defense, the division's special forces battalion is usually grouped with its tank battalion as a mobile and hard-hitting reserve force. In the attack most of the tanks support the main infantry attack, but a company or more would be held back along with the special forces battalion as an exploitation force. The Iraqi Army is not proficient at battlefield reconnaissance, and so the actual infantry attack is used to find weak spots. Once the broad front attack identifies a weak spot, the heavily armed special forces battalion, reinforced with tanks, is committed to break through and exploit.

The Iraqi Army is reported to have six special forces, four of which were formed in August of 1990 immediately after the invasion of Kuwait. As troops of this caliber cannot be created by waving a hand, it is almost certain that the divisions were formed from special forces brigades withdrawn from infantry divisions and some of the corps. Although none of these six divisions have been positively identified in Kuwait, it is possible that some or all of the motorized infantry divisions moving south with the IX Reserve Corps (see Iraqi Deployment section) are in fact special forces divisions.

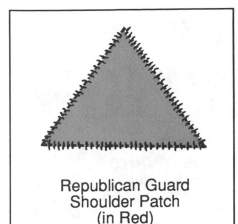

Republican Guard
Shoulder Patch
(in Red)

THE REPUBLICAN GUARD

The Iraqi Republican Guard was originally intended to provide President Saddam Hussein with a body of troops of unquestioning loyalty. As the principal means of presidential succession in Iraq has become coup and murder, these troops were more political than military. They originally consisted of three brigades recruited from Tikrit, Hussein's hometown in northern Iraq.

Although the comparisons between Hitler and Hussein can be pushed too far, the original purpose of the Republican Guard was very similar to the SS, a small, politically reliable paramilitary force intended to serve as the ruler's personal armed bodyguard. Its subsequent growth has been similar as well. Just as the SS later became a significant part of the German armed forces, absorbed a majority of its best equipment, and formed a heavily mechanized *corps d'elite*, so also has the Republican Guard.

In 1986 the Guard began expanding into a major combat force by means of transfers of selected veteran cadres from the regulars and the addition of thousands of politically sympathetic young volunteers, many of them students. By the end of Iraq's war with Iran the Guard had expanded to its current strength: 25 maneuver brigades.

Guard units are lavishly equipped by Iraqi standards. Each brigade is self-contained and includes a full battalion of artillery (18 155mm howitzers) in addition to its brigade mortar battery. Infantry squads are the normal ten men, but each squad has its own light machinegun and RPG-7 rocket launcher (as opposed to one of each per platoon in regular army units). Tank battalions have four companies instead of three (total of 60 tanks instead of 44). Most of the T-72s, T-62s, and BMPs are assigned to Guard units, and the motorized divisions have a number of APCs and extra tanks.

Iraqi guard divisions have the standard 3-brigade organization except for the 5th "Baghdad" division. This division, the permanent garrison of the capital, has four brigades and is sometimes divided into two mini-divisions of two brigades each. If reinforcements for the front were required, the division might be split like this and one mini-division sent while the other remained and guarded the government.

The distinctive insignia of the Iraqi Republican Guard is a red triangle worn as a shoulder patch.

Iraq DESERT SHIELD FACT BOOK

Iraqi Army Equipment:
5500 Main Battle Tanks
1000 IFVs
1000 armored recon vehicles
7000 APCs
3000 towed guns
500 SP guns
4000 air defense guns
350 long-range SAMs
200 multiple rocket launchers
75+ surface to surface missiles
160 armed attack helicopters

**Republican Guard
Order of Battle**
1st Armored Division
    "Hammurabi"
2nd Armored Division
    "Medina"
3rd Mechanized Division
    "Tawakalna"
4th Motorized Division
    "Al Faw"
5th Motorized Division
    "Baghdad"
6th Motorized Division
    "Nebuchadnezzar"
7th Motorized Division
    "Adnan"
8th Special Forces Division

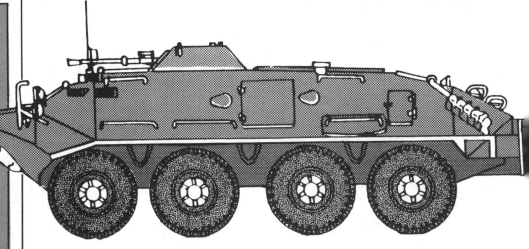

Iraq has approximately 7000 armored personnel carriers of which the most numerous is the Soviet-built BTR 60.

STRUCTURE OF THE ARMY
IRAQI ORGANIZATION

Iraqi corps function as the permanent field headquarters in the Iraqi Army. They have no fixed organization, and they can control a variable number of divisions and separate brigades, depending on their specific missions.

The largest unit in the Iraqi army with a fixed organization is the division. A division consists of three maneuver brigades (infantry, armor, or mechanized), an artillery brigade, and a variety of supporting battalions and companies.

The three principal types of divisions in the Iraqi Army are infantry, mechanized, and armor. The infantry and mechanized organizations are shown in the three accompanying diagrams.

COMBAT UNITS

Each battalion in the division consists of three companies, each of which is in turn made up of three platoons. Tank platoons have 4 tanks (14 in the company, 44 in the battalion). Artillery platoons have two guns, howitzers, or multiple rocket launchers (6 in the battery, as artillery companies are called, 18 in the

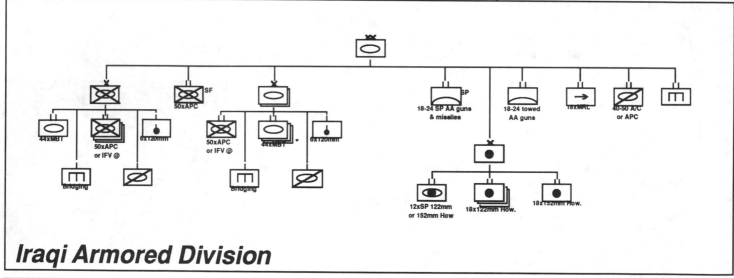

Iraqi Armored Division

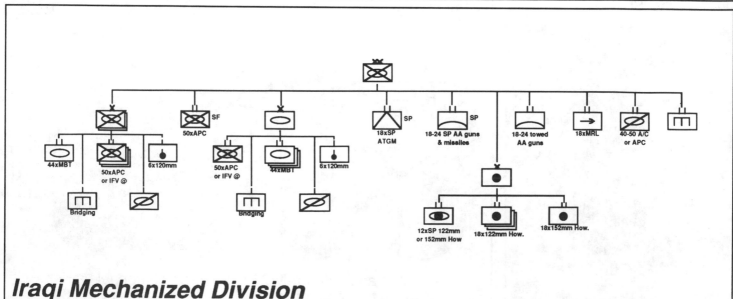

Iraqi Mechanized Division

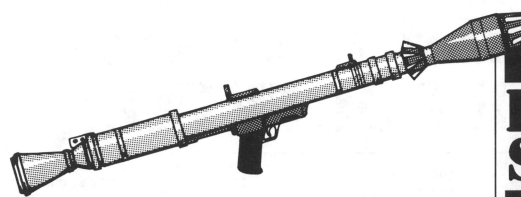

battalion). Infantry platoons have three 10-man rifle squads and a small weapons squad with a light machinegun and an RPG-7 rocket launcher.

In some mechanized units, the company has a 60mm mortar platoon (2 mortars) in addition to its three rifle platoons. Otherwise there are no mortars or heavy weapons in a battalion other than those of the weapons squads in each platoon.

Iraqi Republican Guard units are stronger than this. Each tank battalion has four companies instead of three (60 tanks instead of 44), each company has a platoon of 82mm mortars, and each rifle squad has its own light machinegun and RPG-7. Many special forces units may be organized and equipped similarly.

SUPPORT UNITS

In addition to the combat units shown on the charts, brigades and divisions have a number of non-combat support units which meet basic needs. Each brigade has a supply company and a chemical decontamination platoon. Each division has a supply and transport battalion, a medical battalion, a communication battalion, a military police company, and a chemical decontamination company. All armored or mechanized divisions also have a technical engineering battalion in addition to their combat engineer battalion. This unit contains heavy bridging and road construction equipment needed to sustain division mobility in difficult terrain.

INFANTRY PLATOON FIREPOWER

This chart compares the manpower and weapons of a U.S. mechanized infantry platoon equipped with Bradley IFVs to an Iraqi mechanized platoon equipped with BMP IFVs. Virtually all US infantry is mechanized and mounted in Bradleys. Most Iraqi infantry is leg-mobile, and only about 15% of the mechanized battalions have BMPs; the rest use APCs armed only with machineguns.

Category	U.S.	Iraq
Men	33	36
IFVs	4	4
AR	24	32
GL	7	0
SAW	6	1
GPMG	3	0
ATRL	15	1
ATGM	3	0

Notes: IFV = Infantry Fighting Vehicle (US Bradley with 25mm chaingun and TOW-II launcher, Iraqi BMP-1 with 73mm low velocity gun and AT-3 Sagger launcher), AR = assault rifle (US M16, Iraqi AKM), GL = grenade launcher (US M203), SAW = Squad Automatic Weapon (US M249 SAW, Iraqi RPK), GPMG = General Purpose Machinegun (US M-60), ATRL=Anti-tank Rocket Launcher (US M79 LAW, Iraqi RPG-7), ATGM=Anti-tank Guided Missile (US Dragon).

Iraqi Infantry Division

IRAQI FIGHTING TECHNIQUES
BATTLE DOCTRINE

The Iraqi Army is battle-tested and has developed its own style of combat after years of fighting the Iranians. However, the Iraqis appear to value flexibility, and do not rigidly adhere to fixed battle drills.

Iraqi organizations are flexible and task-oriented. Battalions can be shifted between brigades or even divisions to reinforce a successful drive or shore up crumbling defenses. Cross-attachment of assets is practiced extensively (which is especially important with anti-tank weapons, as the Iraqis are short of these), and the Iraqis practice combined arms warfare at all levels of attack and defense.

Given the large number of infantry formations available, the Iraqis traditionally lead with infantry and then develop with armor. That is, once the infantry attacks discovers a weak spot, the armor piles on, breaks through, and exploits. On defense the Iraqis place a premium of elaborate entrenchments and prepared positions, both for infantry and armor.

Unlike the United States Army, where all troops are expected to be top-notch and mission-capable, troop quality varies greatly within the Iraqi Army. To some extent this is by design. The Iraqis systematically identify high quality troops and concentrate them in elite units. All armored and mechanized units are formed from highly motivated troops and have the best junior officers. Infantry divisions form their own elite units by internally recruiting special forces battalions. Some of the best troops from the regular army elite formations eventually find their way into the Republican Guard.

MOBILE FORCES

Strengths: Heavy divisions and guard divisions are reasonably well-equipped. Although much of the armor is old, there is a lot of it. More importantly, the heavy divisions have high levels of training, morale, and leadership.

Weaknesses: Iraqi tanks are qualitatively badly outmatched by Allied tanks, especially those of the United States. The Iraqis have no experience against an opponent capable of breaking through the front and then conducting a deep, rapid exploitation. The Iranians were primarily an infantry army with tank support; the U.S. Army is completely mechanized or air-mobile. The best defense against a slow-moving infantry army is a thick, solid defensive barrier, such as the one the Iraqis have set up in Kuwait. The only effective defense against hard-hitting mobile forces is a defense in depth.

INFANTRY FORCES

Strengths: The infantry divisions are numerous, have practiced a battle-proven doctrine, and are tenacious in defense. They are masters of entrenchment and will be difficult to dig out of their fortifications.

Weaknesses: Infantry units are poorly equipped and are made up from the scraps of manpower left after numerous elite units have taken the choice recruits. Over half the infantry divisions are truly leg-mobile and would be immobile in the event of hostilities. All of the infantry divisions are critically short of anti-tank weapons at every level.

FIELD ARTILLERY

Strengths: Numerous, well-

trained, and can deliver quick, responsive fire support.

Weaknesses: Six out of every seven field guns are towed instead of self-propelled, which makes them very easy to suppress. When self-propelled guns come under counter-battery fire, they can drive out of the area, redeploy, and begin firing again. The crews of towed guns have no option but to take cover and stay there until the fire lifts. Also, ammunition stacked in the open by towed guns makes them much more vulnerable to destruction by counter-battery fire.

AIR DEFENSE ARTILLERY

Strengths: Units are very numerous and will be a continuing barrier to effective close air support in the forward battle area.

Weaknesses: No experience against a numerous and determined air offensive. Radar-controlled guns and missiles, the most effective systems the Iraqis have, can be jammed by Allied electronic warfare units and destroyed by radar-homing missiles.

COMBAT HELICOPTERS

Strengths: Combat helicopter units are numerous, experienced, and highly proficient. They were repeatedly and successfully used to break up Iranian assaults.

Weaknesses: No training or experience in dealing with an opponent who also employs large numbers of helicopter gunships.

COMMAND CONTROL

Strengths: Command control is very good. Iraq was repeatedly able to mass reserves of aircraft, helicopters, and armor at critical points of the battlefield during the war with Iran. This, much more than the infrequent use of chemical weapons, was the key to Iraqi victory.

Weaknesses: Allied air superiority will make rapid movement of mobile reserves difficult and costly. Iraqi headquarters are vulnerable to air attacks and may be disrupted or destroyed during the critical opening phases of a battle.

IN GENERAL

Strengths: Combat experience has led to high troop morale and confidence. The Iraqis are extremely flexible; if one approach to a problem fails, they will try another. They are innovative and quick to learn. In all probability they would be fighting on the defensive in familiar territory and defending their homeland against a foreign aggressor.

Weaknesses: All units have very poor night fighting skills. Night vision equipment is virtually nonexistent. This was not much of a problem when fighting the Iranians. It may prove to be catastrophic if called upon to fight U.S. troops, who have the best night-vision equipment in the world and are well-trained in night offensive operations.

Reconnaissance and military intelligence are weak. Sometimes ground recon units probe for weak spots; more often weak spots are found by launching broad front infantry attacks. Air reconnaissance is not well-integrated into the intelligence apparatus and will be virtually unavailable (due to Allied air superiority) in the event of a war. In the Iran-Iraq War, Iran built a 30-mile causeway through the swamps in Iraqi territory without Iraq noticing

Iraq
DESERT SHIELD
FACT BOOK

until it was nearly completed.

Logistical support is very poor, and cannot keep up with the tempo of modern operations. Instead, supplies are stockpiled for an operation over the course of months and then consumed in days when an attack is launched.

Iraqi infantry brigades usually entrench along a 15-kilometer front, with the front line consisting of three triangular battalion forts at 5-kilometer intervals. Each fort is an equilateral triangle about two kilometers across, with each side formed by a bulldozed wall of packed dirt or sand from two to four meters in height. All of the battalion's vehicles are parked in the middle of the fort.

The actual fighting positions are on the points of the fort, with one company position at each corner. Each of the company positions consists of three platoon forts in a triangular layout, and each platoon complex consists of three squad positions, also in a triangular layout. The company forts are about 700 meters across, the platoon forts about 200 meters. Each squad fighting position is designed for all-around fire, and is usually built from packed earth reinforced by steel mesh and/or concrete. Each sub-unit places its command post and heavy weapons in the center of of the fighting position.

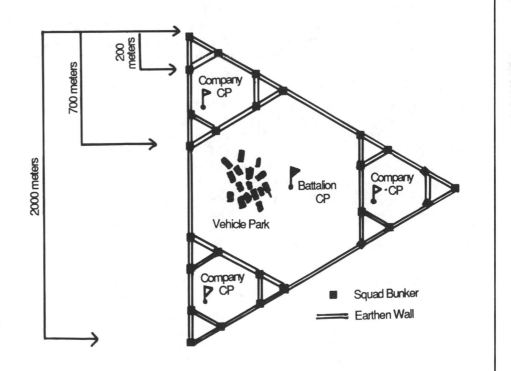

Each fort is surrounded by barbed wire and minefields, when sufficient engineering supplies are available. The Iraqi forts in Kuwait are fronted by three belts of mines, each separated by an anti-tank ditch. Barrels of gasoline are placed in many of the ditches with remote explosive charges that can be command-detonated from the Iraqi positions.

IRAQI TRIANGULAR BATTALION FORTS

THE CUTTING EDGE
IRAQI ARMOR

Although armor cannot win a battle by itself, armored fighting vehicles (AFVs) form the core of any offensive force on the modern battlefield, especially in largely open ground such as the Arabian Peninsula. The Iraqi armored forces are the best trained and led in their army and can be expected to offer stiff resistance.

T-55 MAIN BATTLE TANK

The T-55, despite its considerable age, remains in service with armies worldwide in large numbers. Although it is obsolete today, when it appeared it was the most dangerous tank in any nation's arsenal, and caused a complete revolution in tank design.

Before T-55 became operational, most armies adopted a mix of light tanks for scouting, large numbers of general-purpose medium tanks as the workhorses of the armored and mechanized formations, and a small number of expensive heavy tanks (mounting the biggest tank gun available and the strongest armor) to lead the breakthrough against enemy armored units.

What made the T-55 unique was that it had the armament and firepower of a heavy tank but was designed for cheap mass production. It replaced both medium and heavy tanks in the force structure, and was the first true *Main Battle Tank*.

Virtually all MBTs designed since then have followed this pattern, and the NATO nations mounted several stop-gap interim programs to con-

vert many of their existing medium tanks to MBTs. For example, the British at that time fielded the Centurion medium tank with a 90mm gun and the Conqueror heavy tank with a 120mm gun. They soon developed the L-7 105mm tank gun (specifically designed to defeat the frontal armor of the T-55), retrofitted it to the Centurion, increased the Centurion's frontal armor, and retired their Conquerors from service.

In its day the T-55 was an extraordinary tank. Today it would be badly outmatched in a tank duel by almost any Allied tank. It can still provide yeoman service against infantry and light mechanized forces, and the sheer numbers available make that threat doubly significant. However, Iraqi shortages of anti-tank weapons at every level mean that they would have to commit their armor against an Allied mechanized breakthrough, and that means committing them to tank-versus-tank fights where they will be at a considerable disadvantage.

The Chinese T-59 is an austere copy of the T-55, and lacks a number of "luxuries" (such as powered turret traverse) that most armies consider necessities. Recent production examples exported to other countries have shown signs of very poor quality control, including critical components such as the turret ring and traversing gears.

Specifications

Weight:	36 tons
Road Speed:	48 k/h
Gun:	100mm D-10T2S
Rounds Carried:	43
Armor:	200mm
On Hand:	2,500 basic T-55
	1,500 Chinese T-59

T-62 MAIN BATTLE TANK

The T-62 is a simple follow-on to the T-55. It uses a slightly modified turret to accept the more powerful U-5TS 115mm smoothbore, the first adopted by the Soviets.

T-62 was a disappointing tank, swiftly replaced by the T-64 and its cousin, the T-72. At a time when Western tank design was rapidly closing the lead established by the T-55, T-62 was virtually no improvement over its predecessor in mobility or protection, and only a marginal improvement in firepower. The 115mm gun has better penetration, and accuracy is fairly good out to about 1200 meters. After that, however, its accuracy plummets. While T-55 was one of the most powerful tanks in Europe in its day, T-62 did not compare favorably to early versions of the U.S. M-60, and is markedly inferior to the M60A3.

That notwithstanding, T-62 is better than T-55 and forms the bulk of the "modern" tanks in Iraqi service. Relatively few T-62s were exported. Most were shipped to the Arab states in the early 1970s. Iraqi T-62s are concentrated in the elite Republican Guard divisions.

Specifications

Weight:	36.5 tons
Road Speed:	50 k/h
Gun:	115mm U-5TS
Rounds Carried:	40
Armor:	200mm
Number on Hand:	1,000

T-72 MAIN BATTLE TANK

Although better than earlier Soviet tanks, the basic T-72 production model is poorly protected by contemporary standards, and the fact that the fuel and ammo are packed tightly together in the cramped hull makes a high percentage of hits catastrophic kills.

Recognizing this failing, the Soviets have progressively increased the armor on later production versions of the T-72. The T-72G model has a visibly thicker hull and turret front. (The noticeable turret bulge in the front has led this variant to be nicknamed the "Dolly Parton" by U.S. tankers.) This vehicle has estimated frontal protection equivalent to 350mm of armor plate.

The latest variant, the T-72M, has even thicker turret armor (upping its protection to 400mm and earning it the nickname "Dolly Parton II"), applique armor on the turret roof, and a laser range finder.

The majority of Iraq's T-72s are the early production version. There are probably no more than 300 of the T-72M version on hand.

The T-72 mounts a large smoothbore gun which comes close to overloading the small chassis. As the Soviets like to build their tanks small (so they can fit through existing Soviet railway tunnels), they couldn't fit the gun and a full crew in the vehicle. Consequently, they substituted an automatic loading mechanism for the fourth crew member.

The autoloader used is essentially a scaled-up version of the autoloader on the 73mm gun of the BMP-1 infantry fighting vehicle. That particular autoloader was notorious for snagging the gunner's fatigues and trying to load his arm into the gun, and it turns out that the loader on the T-72 has the same nasty tendency. Given the small number of T-72s in service, however, it is likely that their picked crews are well-trained and careful to avoid accidents such as this.

A continuing problem in Soviet tank design for nearly thirty years has been disappointing main gun accuracy, and the T-72 continues that dubious tradition. Because of the high velocity and flat trajectory, accuracy is good out to 1500 meters, but falls off drastically after that.

Specifications

Weight:	41 tons
Road Speed:	50 k/h
Gun:	125mm
Rounds Carried:	40
Armor:	250mm
	350mm in T-72G
	400mm in T-72M
Number on Hand:	up to 1500

BMP-1
Infantry Fighting Vehicle

The Soviet BMP (*Bronevaya Maschina Piekhota*, or Armored Vehicle, Infantry) was the world's first genuine infantry fighting vehicle (IFV), and most nations have scrambled to follow suit. The German *Marder*, British Warrior, French AMX-10P, Dutch AIFV, and American M2 Bradley all trace their origin to the appearance of the BMP in Red Square in November of 1967.

Although the concept of a highly capable infantry carrier remains controversial, it is clearly here to stay for the foreseeable future. What the BMP is designed to do is combine a specialized firepower support vehicle with a traditional armored troop carrier. This allows the squad to travel under armor on the road (which makes it more difficult for artillery to disrupt the forward movement of the unit). Then when the infantry dismounts for the attack, the BMP follows and provides additional firepower as needed. In effect, it enables the squad to carry around a recoilless rifle and an ATGM launcher, plus a fair amount of ammunition for both, without burdening the riflemen in the squad.

One thing that the BMP was never intended to do was carry its rifle squad forward into the area swept by enemy direct fire; its armor is proof only against artillery fragments. Its superficial resemblance to a tank has fooled many uninformed observers (and a surprising number of people who ought to know better) into thinking that it was a heavy assault vehicle. It is not.

Most of Iraq's BMPs are concentrated in the mechanized brigades of the Republican Guard.

Specifications

Weight:	14 tons
Road Speed:	70 k/h
Gun:	73mm smoothbore
Missile:	AT-3 Sagger
Passengers:	8 infantrymen
Rounds Carried:	
	40 cannon rounds
	5 missiles
Armor:	15-20mm.
Number on Hand:	1,000.

CHEMICAL BIOLOGICAL NUCLEAR
SPECIAL WEAPONS

One persistent concern about Iraq's military capability is the area of so-called *weapons of mass destruction*, a term coined by the Soviets as a catch-all for nuclear, chemical, and biological warfare. As Iraq has a number of short range and intermediate range missiles, there are concerns that it may be able to conduct attacks against civilian targets throughout the region.

CHEMICAL WARFARE

Chemical weapons refer to poisonous gas. There are three general types of poisonous gas used by military forces: blood agents, blister agents, and nerve agents.

MOPP Suit

Blood agents enter the blood stream after they are inhaled and literally poison the victim.

Blister agents will cause severe skin lesions and, if inhaled, will damage the lungs.

Nerve agents (or nerve gas) attack the central nervous system and can either enter the system by inhalation or by absorption through the skin.

All three types of chemical agents are potentially lethal.

Iraq has a total of 400 tons of lethal chemical agents on hand, divided between Tabun and Sarin (two nerve agents developed by, but never used by, the Germans in World War II) and Mustard Gas (the most common blister agent, originally used in World War I). These are held at four main storage facilities, located at Karbala, Al Fallujah, Baija, and Samarra.

Chemical Protection: The most basic protection against chemical agents is the gas mask. A mask will not protect troops against the painful effects of skin contact with blister agents, but it will keep the soldier alive and let him or her exit the area of chemical contamination.

There are reports that Iraq is also trying to manufacture hydrogen cyanide, a lethal blood agent which has the additional effect of eating through the filters of gas masks. The current U.S. gas mask (unlike earlier models) allows the soldier to change the filter without removing his or her mask.

Nerve agents in their liquid form can be absorbed through the skin even if a mask is worn. Most allied troops are issued with atropine, however, an antidote to nerve gas. This is issued to U.S. troops in the form of an autoinjector. This is pressed against the arm or leg and the needle automatically injects the drug into the soldier.

Although masks and atropine will allow troops to escape from area of contamination by nerve or blister agents, they do not allow a unit to function in that environment. In order to do that, troops must either put on their MOPP (Mission Operative Protective Posture) suits or be in a chemically protected vehicle. The most common form of vehicle chemical protection is an overpressure system such as that found on the M1A1.

Limits on Usefulness: Chemical warfare is less effective against

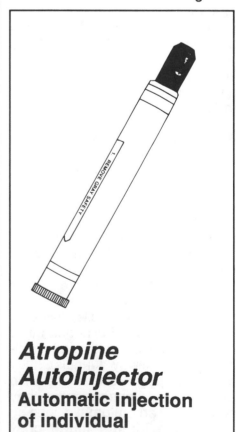

Atropine AutoInjector
Automatic injection of individual nerve gas antidote.

BIOLOGICAL WARFARE

Very little is known about Iraq's biological warfare program, except that research is ongoing and seems to be concentrating on strains of Rabbit Fever. Recent reports have also indicated that some work in anthrax is being done. The biological weapons development center is at Salman Pak, southeast of Baghdad.

mechanized troops than against leg infantry, as troops obtain a degree of protection from their vehicles (and the ability to quickly leave contaminated areas). Most of the allied forces are mechanized.

Nerve gas is actually delivered in liquid form, and can only be absorbed through the skin while liquid. At high temperatures, however, it quickly volatilizes into gas. In its gaseous state it is still lethal if inhaled but is absorbed through the skin at a slower rate, giving troops time to leave contaminated areas.

For chemical weapons to be effective, they must be used when atmospheric conditions are favorable. As these conditions are rare in the Middle East, allied NBC (Nuclear, Biological, Chemical) intelligence officers can predict probable employment opportunities and take precautions.

Iraq has never used gas on an enemy which had adequate chemical defenses or the capacity for an effective response. For that matter, no nation on earth since World War I has done so. The U.S. Army is one of the best-equipped and best-trained armies in the world to survive and respond to chemical attacks.

Delivering the Goods: Although there are persistent rumors that the Iraqis have been working to deploy a chemical warhead for their battlefield missile systems, there is no hard evidence that they have succeeded in doing so. Unless and until they do, the main delivery means will be by 152mm and 155mm artillery shells.

NUCLEAR WEAPONS

It is impossible to say for certain how close Iraq is to developing a nuclear warhead, but there is no question that Iraq is working toward that goal. U.S. intelligence believes that Iraq can assemble two weapons within two years and begin mass production sometime after that. Israeli Defense Minister Moshe Arens, however, disagrees, and has suggested that if technology can be kept from Iraq, then development of a warhead might be postponed indefinitely.

Nuclear weapons can be built either from plutonium or enriched uranium. The Iraqis had a working nuclear reactor capable of making plutonium but the Israeli Air Force destroyed it in a controversial bombing mission years ago.

The alternative is enriched uranium, a more difficult proposition. Iraq currently has at least 55 pounds of enriched uranium on hand, however, enough for one or two warheads. This was purchased in the early 1980s (half from the Soviet Union, half from France) ostensibly to fuel a nuclear power station. It has never been used for that purpose, but also had not been made into a bomb as of the last international inspection of the material about a year ago.

Iraq has also been mining uranium in the northern Gara Mountains (in Kurdistan) since early 1989. Uranium by itself is useless unless it can be enriched by gas centrifuge equipment which, until recently, was thought to be unavailable to Iraq. It has recently been discovered, however, that Iraq purchased gas centrifuge machines from a German firm and has established an enrichment facility near Mosul.

Although Iraq's short-term ability to develop a warhead is questionable, it clearly has developed the infrastructure needed to support a long-term program for the manufacture of large numbers of nuclear warheads.

Iraq

DESERT SHIELD

FACT BOOK

Chemical Hysteria

To an extent, the American public has become fixated on Iraq's potential for chemical warfare. Certainly the attention paid to it in the news media, while appropriate, has had the (probably unintended) effect of exaggerating its military potential. Although no military threat should be ignored or dismissed, several points about this issue deserve emphasizing.

● Iraq has limited stocks of chemical agents and very limited delivery systems. Most, if not all, of its missiles lack the capability to deliver gas, and almost all of them have very small payloads (100 to 300 pounds).

● The environment in Kuwait, Saudi Arabia, and Southern Iraq is very unfavorable for the effective employment of chemical weapons.

● The Allies possess overwhelming retaliatory capability, which will make any opponent think twice before using chemical weapons.

● Chemical weapons are the *only* weapons on the modern battlefield which a soldier can absolutely defeat 100% of the time by being alert, following his training, and using his equipment properly. Bullets, bombs, and shells are random killers; gas kills only the unwary and unprepared.

ORDER OF BATTLE
IRAQI DEPLOYMENTS

The following assessment of Iraqi troop dispositions is based on the best open source material available at the time of this writing (December 1990).

1. BAGHDAD

30,000 men
180 tanks
120 guns
1 Guards motorized infantry division (5th "Baghdad")
1 air assault brigade

This is the regular garrison of Baghdad. This is a four-brigade division and the unit is sometimes broken into two mini-divisions.

2. MOVING SOUTH FROM BAGHDAD

250,000 men
750 tanks
650 guns
IX Reserve Corps headquarters
6 Reserve Infantry Divisions
1 Reserve Tank Division
5 motorized infantry divisions

The Iraqi government has announced that these troops are to reinforce the defenders of Kuwait, but this may be deliberate disinformation. Kuwait is already packed with troops and the Iraqis will have difficulty supplying more within that confined space. Also, as more and more troops are piled into Kuwait, an attack north of Kuwait to cut them off looks more and more inviting. Nevertheless, by late December additional infantry units of the IX Reserve Corps were arriving in Kuwait and began deploying to thicken the ground defenses.

There is a strong likelihood that at least some of the troops moving with the IX Reserve Corps will be used to reinforce the defenses along the Iraqi-Saudi frontier northwest of Kuwait. Arguably the best positions for them would be entrenched along the south bank of the Euphrates River at strategic road junctions, such as As Samawah and An Najaf. They would be easy to supply there and they would provide needed operational depth to the Iraqi defenses, particularly along the northwestern flank.

Some or all of the divisions identified above as motorized infantry may in fact be special forces divisions.

3. WEST OF BAGHDAD

50,000 men
250 tanks
180 guns
II Guards Corps Headquarters
3 Guards motorized infantry divisions (4th, 6th, 7th)

These troops cover a number of strategic installations in the Karbala-Habaniya area. A major allied drive north across the desert from Rafha would encounter this corps as the final reserve before Baghdad.